What Adults Need to Know about Kids and Substance Use

Dealing with Alcohol, Tobacco, and Other Drugs

Katharine Sadler, M.Ed.

SEARCH INSTITUTE PRESS

What Adults Need to Know about Kids and Substance Use: Dealing with Alcohol, Tobacco, and Other Drugs
Katharine Sadler, M.Ed.

Search Institute Press, Minneapolis, MN
Copyright © 2011 by Search Institute

10 9 8 7 6 5 4 3 2 1
Printed on acid-free paper in the United States of America

Search Institute
615 First Avenue Northeast, Suite 125
Minneapolis, MN 55413
www.search-institute.org
612-376-8955 • 877-240-7251

ISBN-13: 978-1-57482-495-7

Credits
Editor: Kate Brielmaier
Book Design: Mayfly Design
Production Supervisor: Mary Ellen Buscher

**Library of Congress
Cataloging-in-Publication Data**
Sadler, Katharine.
    What adults need to know about kids and substance use : dealing with alcohol, tobacco, and other drugs /
Katharine Sadler.
    p. cm.
    Includes bibliographical references and index.
    ISBN-13: 978-1-57482-495-7 (pbk. : alk. paper)
    ISBN-10: 1-57482-495-3 (pbk. : alk. paper)
    1. Teenagers—Substance use—Prevention.
2. Children—Substance use—Prevention.
3. Teenagers—Drug use—Prevention.
4. Children—Drug use—Prevention. 5. Child rearing. 6. Parenting. I. Title.
    HV4999.Y68S24 2011
    362.29'170835—dc22
                                2010048184

Contents

Introduction

IT CAN BE DIFFICULT TO TELL IF A YOUNG PERSON IS EXPERIMENTING with substances. Kids don't always show obvious signs of substance abuse, and we do not have a way of predicting who will experiment with alcohol, tobacco, or other drugs in the future. Substance misuse and addiction do not discriminate against culture, income level, or race. Some teens will experiment and walk away; others *can't* walk away. There are teens who are surrounded by protective factors and could be poster children for developmental success, yet they may still fall prey to drug abuse. There are also teens who carry several risk factors who survive and thrive. There is no rule of thumb.

What we do know is that providing assets and protective factors gives our teens a better fighting chance against many adversities, drugs included. Trying to guess which youth will abuse drugs and which won't is like trying to predict who will get cancer and who will stay healthy. But just as there are things we can do to prevent cancer through education and by taking care of ourselves, there are things we can do to help youth through the struggles of substance abuse issues.

As kids experiment—and statistics tell us many of them will—we must be armed to help them. If we let ourselves believe that substance abuse only affects a certain kind of kid, or can be easily spotted just by looking, then many youth we have a chance to help will fall through the cracks. Youth who abuse drugs may look like they belong on a late-night reality show about inner-city thugs. They may be loners or group themselves with others who listen to ear-splitting music and care only about their own subculture. But they may also be honor roll students who ingest prescription medicine for attention deficit disorder to stay awake all night to study, or varsity athletes who take huge quantities of dietary supplements to enhance their performance. Or they may just be ordinary kids at a party, drinking beer and smoking marijuana.

Snap Judgments

I remember a moment when I judged too quickly. I was disturbed while watching an intimidating group dressed in outlandish black outfits and black nail polish gather together outside the cafeteria during lunch. I felt surprise at my own narrow-mindedness when they opened their Bibles for a study group.

We also need to expand our idea of *kids*, *youth*, or *teens*. Substance abuse prevention has focused on teens in middle and high school, but the specific teen years of 13 through 19 are too narrow a section of the population. Children as young as 11 and 12 years old are experimenting with over-the-counter drugs, and college students are using ADHD medicine to get an edge on studies. When this book refers to *kids*, *youth*, or *teens*, it refers to a wide range of young people who have the ability and desire to experiment with substances. That wide age range is also connected to the development of the brain—recent research states that the brain is not fully developed until we are around 24 years of age.[1]

It's Not *What* They Use, but *Why*

Common substances abused by youth include nicotine and alcohol. These are considered gateway drugs, or substances that often introduce users to other substances. Other drugs commonly abused by youth include over-the-counter medicine and prescription drugs. Inhalants such as aerosols and household cleaners are being abused at a quickly growing rate. Research shows that illegal substances are less commonly abused by this generation of young people; rather, abuse of illegal drugs tends to be by adult users and addicts.[2]

But we don't need to keep ahead of what is being smoked, swallowed, injected, absorbed, or snorted. Something new will always be on the horizon. People will continually find new ways to seek a "high." For example, a recent trend is legally smoking certain types of incense. "K2" and "Spice" contain a combination of synthetic chemicals that cause the same effects as THC (the mind-altering drug in marijuana). When these are either banned from the market or considered unworthy of the risk, there will be another untested chemical combination to take their place. So while it is important to note which substance is the chemical of choice (alcohol, marijuana, prescriptions, or household chemicals), it is more important to get a grasp on the reasons for a teen's substance abuse. By finding the root causes, we may be able to help change cognitive thinking and build a web of protective factors around the individual teen.

We know how to handle a failed test, bad study habits, or a fight. Those conversations are easier to start with parents than the one that links a child with substance abuse. The situation is difficult from the point of view of the counselor, teacher, or youth worker, and from the point of view of the parent. There are so many different reasons and situations that bring young people to abuse drugs. Study after study will blame one effect or another as the strongest reason that alcohol and other substances are abused, but in most cases it is not just one reason but a combination of them. Whatever the reasons, though, we are not helpless. We have the skills and information to make a difference when a young person comes to us about a drug problem

I recently spoke to a school counselor. When I mentioned that there are telltale signs that a teen is abusing substances, I could see the questions coming. He asked how teachers can be trained to look for the evidence. He wanted to know how to identify at-risk youth. Many schools and youth programs don't offer much information for their staff about these topics because they become overwhelmed by the magnitude of the problem, eventually throwing up their hands and saying, "They're all at risk" and leaving it at that. But it is possible to break down information into digestible bites, and it is possible to envision potential scenarios and ways to respond. This book is designed to do just that.

How to Use This Book

Section I is about the why and the where of teenage drug use: Chapter 1 explains factors that affect drug use—family and home dynamics, social pressure, genetics— and Chapter 2 discusses where kids go to get drugs. Section II is about being proactive and reactive: Chapter 3 talks about prevention tactics with adults and within school and the community. Chapter 4 offers advice about what to do during specific scenarios, such as when a young person comes to us about her drug use—or about her friend's or parent's drug use. Chapter 5 covers ways to talk to parents and other adults, situations in which the authorities should be alerted, and how we can reach the best possible outcome in any scenario. Chapter 6 is about drug treatment and how to work with young people who are going through it. Finally, Section III is about specific drugs, including their physical and emotional effects and ways to identify the signs of their use. Chapter 7 discusses over-the-counter (or minimally restricted) substances such as inhalants, cough medicine, and antihistamines, while Chapter 8 focuses on legally available but more carefully restricted substances such as tobacco, alcohol, and prescription medication. Chapter 9 is about illegal drugs like marijuana, heroin, club drugs, and methamphetamines.

Using this book, the prevention resources available in your community, and your own innate skills and talents, it is possible to make a difference in the lives of young people who are affected by substance use.

References

1. Jessie Breyer and Ken C. Winters, "Adolescent Brain Development: Implications for Drug Use Prevention." Minneapolis: Center for Substance Abuse Research, Department of Psychiatry, University of Minnesota, & Mentor USA, 2004. www.mentorfoundation.org/pdfs/prevention_perspectives/19.pdf.

2. L. D. Johnston, P. M. O'Malley, J. G. Bachman, and J. E. Schulenberg, *Monitoring the Future: National Survey Results on Drug Use, 1975–2008: Volume I, Secondary School Students* (NIH Publication No. 09-7402), Bethesda, MD: National Institute on Drug Abuse, 2009.

Section I

Teens and Substance Use

Chapter 1

Factors That Affect Alcohol, Tobacco, and Other Drug Use

MANY OF US EXPERIMENTED WITH DRUGS AS TEENAGERS (EVEN IF WE don't admit it to the teens we work with) and probably stopped at cigarettes, alcohol, or marijuana. Some of us had to deal with the challenge of harder substances. The fact that you are reading this means you passed through the experience—not necessarily untouched or unharmed, but you are on the other side of your "research."

According to a national survey in 2009, 72.5 percent of students in grade 12 have had at least one drink of alcohol.[1] And it is safe to say that, like us, most teens who try alcohol or other substances will also arrive on the other side of their experimentation unscathed and hopefully wiser for the experience. However, since we are unable to see into the future, we cannot be certain which teens will not be harmed. Genetics, social pressure, and family dynamics have all been noted as factors in why teens move from experimentation to drug abuse.

Family and Home Dynamics

Drug abuse is often a multigenerational issue. Some parents—and even grandparents—are using drugs recreationally and abusing alcohol regularly. A child who grows up in this environment may see that behavior as natural. We may be his teacher or mentor and can spout facts about the dangers of substance use until we are blue in the face, but the people whom this child trusts, who care for him and love him, usually prevail as the norm in his mind. While we may see the child for an hour daily, he has a lifetime with family members who may think differently from us. When we don't know the circumstances that surround the student, we may unknowingly build a wall by stating things that contradict what goes on at home. While we can tell him one thing, his family experience says otherwise.

Who Are You Going to Believe?

A first-grade teacher I knew felt it was her responsibility to teach her students that Santa Claus didn't exist. She gave exact details on the origins of St. Nick and Father Christmas, but one student chose to believe otherwise and had trouble trusting his teacher after that declaration. In his world, Santa had made a very convincing visit to his home and his parents referred to the red-suited man as a real person. His personal family experiences overruled anything the teacher could say and caused a struggle in his willingness to learn from her.

We cannot argue with a teen's interpretation of the dangers of substance use or her interpretation of the truth in reference to family. Some teens have seen adults in their lives who abuse drugs and seem unharmed for the practice. Teens may watch parents who drink to the point of intoxication nightly and still go to work the next day—functional alcoholics. When adults appear unaltered by or face few consequences for the misuse of substances, many teens foresee little harm and are more likely to use themselves.

Family turmoil can also bring on the desire to relieve stress through recreational use of substances. For some it becomes a way to have control over the challenges of home. It can numb the negative feelings that come from knowing that home is unsecure. In this instance, substances are used as a coping mechanism. Some teens can find examples of this survival tool within the walls of their home. Guardians may model how substance abuse can be used to get through a tough situation. The adults may even share methods and substances. Teens are exposed to the present and immediate relief without knowing the short- and long-term effects.

Family structure can also play a part in substance abuse. Gone are the days when one parent stayed home while the other worked. Single-parent households and two-parent households where both parents work are the norm now, and the teens we work with during the day may go home to an empty house where adult supervision is nonexistent. Sometimes that means the teen has ample opportunity to "get into mischief." Other times it means he has greater responsibilities. He may go home to help brothers and sisters off the bus and start dinner. His chores may include laundry, cooking, and putting fed and bathed siblings to bed. Chores and responsibilities can help teens mature and see the life of responsibility that adults accept, but a teen who finds it a challenge to meet both school and home obligations may find solace in drugs and alcohol. Alleviating stress is a necessary part of life, but choosing a good method by which to do this can be difficult.

Different Priorities

"I couldn't believe I stood by and watched my husband hand a marijuana joint to my three teenage stepsons. I felt so helpless. The electric company had just shut the lights off. I knew I should say something but couldn't think of what to say."

The boys' stepmother added that she did not feel she had the authority to tackle the situation. She was certain that confronting her husband would not convince him to change what he was doing at that moment. In her eyes, the damage was done and it was a waste of an argument. "It wouldn't change things and it was wrong to attack my husband in front of the children." More important to her was a calm house and their need for electricity.

Genetics

There is a lot of new research on genetics and drug dependency. Discoveries have found that there is a correlation between the two, but there is no conclusive evidence of the role genetic factors play in alcohol or drug addiction. The exact determination of DNA involvement is difficult when factoring in an environment that supports substance abuse and other risk behaviors. It is the same old argument of nature versus nurture. When a parent abuses substances and a child grows up around this behavior, the parent is promoting drug use by example. The parent may also have a genetic predisposition to addiction and pass that on to her child. Environment and a genetic inclination (confirmed by the parent's addictive use) can both play roles in substance abuse.

Culture

Attitudes toward substance use vary widely across cultures and countries. What is commonplace in one part of the world may be against the law in another. Four-teen-year-olds are allowed to drink beer with their parents in Germany, but one has to be 19 to purchase alcohol in most Canadian provinces, and in Saudi Arabia alcohol is illegal at any age. Heroin use is carefully regulated but legal in Switzerland as part of a treatment program for addicts, and marijuana is legal for medical use in several countries and some U.S. states. The use of peyote for religious ceremonies is allowed for members of the Native American Church, but not for anyone else in the United States.

Of course, people must obey the laws of the country and state they are in: a 15-year-old from Germany can't drink in the United States, and a person from California can't use medical marijuana in Singapore. But cultural expectations and norms are not easy to dismiss, particularly when they come into direct conflict.

When immigrants arrive in a new country, they bring with them cultural traditions that are a deeply ingrained part of who they are. Not only are their children being exposed to a completely different society, but their sense of their own culture also is being tested. Things that were the status quo are now under scrutiny. That 15-year-old German is suddenly being told that he's not old enough to deal with the consequences of drinking, even though teens younger than he is are allowed to drink "back home." The student from Saudi Arabia is suddenly in a place where alcohol use is accepted (or even encouraged). Frustration and misunderstanding can be the result.

Social Pressure

Social pressure can have both positive and negative effects. Good peer pressure can keep some teens in after-school programs or on the basketball team. Negative peer pressure can push teens to seek high-risk activities for acceptance.

Many times, children who are friends in elementary and middle school will have no relationship with each other by the end of high school. It's a time when fitting in means succumbing to certain teen norms, and the pressure on relationships can mean that friendships don't survive. But choosing to end a friendship based on the actions of the other person is difficult. Add to this the childlike trust a youth has in friends, the lack of logic and reasoning skills marked by her age, the investment in time, the great memories they have in common, and the fear and loneliness that come with ending a relationship, and a teen has very powerful reasons to sustain a friendship. Sometimes it's more overwhelming to end the bond than to follow the friend through her destructive behavior.

Those who choose to maintain that link in the face of destructive behavior may do so at a terrible price. Teens have noble ideas of saving a friend, thinking that the friendship will be easily salvageable when a friend "gets done doing stupid things." They have the ability to overlook bad habits, and the naive belief that a friendship can be maintained without negative repercussions. Living above the influence of drugs while maintaining a friendship with someone who uses is not easy. Groups will demean those who stand out due to their separate attitudes and degrade them for not participating.

Different interests and values develop rapidly, and with that may come new friends and choices. When a teen feels too challenged or alienated by a certain group, he may migrate toward one that is more comfortable. These new people bring with them new values and opinions.

At an age when friends become more important to a teen than parental interaction, these peers may endorse high-risk behaviors that include substance abuse. The pressure to use comes alongside the need for acceptance in a group setting. Teens are often more willing to take a high-risk challenge when in the safety of friends. There is a sense of belonging when a teen who abuses substances links with others who use drugs, in the same way that another teen may feel a sense of accomplishment and belonging through school activity or work relationships. It is their community. It is their world.

While some teens may feel this pressure by choosing whether or not to try a substance, the ringleader is also facing similar pressure. The instigator feels that when he convinces others to join in, he has their acceptance and is not alone in his negative behavior. He has less guilt about his choice to use and less fear of retribution by peers and adults.

Addiction

It is unethical, not to mention illegal, to conduct substance abuse experiments on adolescents, so we know little about how a young brain reacts to alcohol or other drugs. Addiction tendencies and genetic predispositions to addiction can play key roles in substance abuse, but the extent to which these are involved is unknown.

We do know that the brain is not fully developed until a person is in her midtwenties. Scientists also suggest that any one of us has a potential for addiction.[2] Our brain chemistry is so carefully formulated that substances such as alcohol, inhalants, prescription drugs, and illicit drugs can make changes in its stability. And it's not just substances that cause chemical changes: other positive feelings from outside sources such as food and relationships can bring increased activity in our "reward pathways." However, for the most part, these do not create the negative aftereffects that substances produce. Combine the fragility of the brain chemistry with the immature brain of a teen, and substances can have serious potential consequences. Many different surveys show that teens who abuse alcohol before 14 years of age are far more likely to have alcohol-related issues as adults. And, depending on how a teen's brain is "wired," what may be mere "experimentation" for one teen can become a full-blown addiction for another.

Performance Enhancement

In this case, *performance enhancement* refers to both mental and physical gains from various drugs. In a 2007 survey, 6.4 percent of college students reported that they abused Adderall (ADHD medication). It is the most commonly abused prescription drug among this group. Adderall is a stimulant young people use to stay awake during periods of heavy studies. Students who are facing pressure to perform in school, excel at tests, and succeed in college programs may be tempted to take a substance that enables them to stay awake and focused in order to gain an edge. According to the national survey of Drug Use and Health, full-time college students were twice as likely to use Adderall nonmedically in the past year as those who had not been in college at all or were only part-time students.[3] Adderall and drugs like it are called *prescription stimulants* and usually contain methylphenidate, which is sold under brand names such as Ritalin, Concerta, Metadate, and Methylin.

Anabolic steroids can be used for physical enhancement, but they are not as widely used as many other prescription drugs. They are usually used by teens to gain size and muscle mass, and while that may be the long-term desire, anabolic steroids have serious physical side effects and do not provide instant gratification as many other substances do.

Risk Factors—and Protective Factors

Risk factors play a role in the susceptibility of youth to substance abuse. According to a study by Hawkins, Catalano, and Miller, there are certain well-established risk factors that have a stronger link to alcohol abuse beyond those already mentioned:

- Economic and social deprivation
- Availability of drugs

- Community laws and norms favorable toward drug use
- Transitions and mobility
- Neighborhood disorganization
- Early and persistent problem behaviors
- Academic failure
- Low degree of commitment to school
- Peer rejection in elementary school
- Alienation and rebelliousness[4]

When you look at the list it can feel overwhelming. How are we supposed to help fix "peer rejection in elementary school" when the student we have is 16 years old? What can we do about economic deprivation and community norms? We can't affect these. We will never move the needle on poverty data by helping one single student out of her circumstances. That's not the essential goal. Increasing protective factors for all young people is the goal.

Building protective factors is a proven method of prevention. Protective factors are positive contributions to a child's life. They are built and sustained through parents and community. Caring and nurturing adults and teachers and the importance of youth to the community can reduce risk-taking behaviors. A sense of belonging and participation in supportive religious settings may play constructive roles toward keeping teens from drug use. We don't have control over many of the particular contributions such as economic deprivation and single parenting, but protective factors, or the lack thereof, can influence why some teens abuse substances and others abstain from use.

The good news is that there are many protective factors that can decrease a teen's risks for alcohol and drug use.

The 40 Developmental Assets®

Search Institute, a nonprofit research group, has identified 40 protective factors that teens can draw on. The 40 Developmental Assets describe qualities and experiences that are crucial to positive youth development. They range from external supports like a caring school climate and positive family communication to internal characteristics such as school engagement and a sense of purpose.

Search Institute has done extensive research, reviewing more than 1,200 studies from major bodies of literature, including prevention, resilience, and adolescent development, to identify what young people need to thrive. Institute researchers have documented that young people who are healthy, whether they come from the poorest or the wealthiest environments and from diverse ethnic and cultural groups, have certain meaningful elements in their lives. Researchers identified eight categories that describe these elements:

- The solid presence of **support** from others;
- A feeling of **empowerment**;
- A clear understanding of **boundaries and expectations**;
- Varied opportunities for **constructive use of time**;
- A strong **commitment to learning**;
- An appreciation of **positive values**;
- Sound **social competencies**; and
- A personal sense of **positive identity**.

Moreover, research conducted by Search Institute consistently shows that the strengths described within these categories provide a solid foundation for positive development and academic success, and that their presence helps protect youth from engaging in risky behavior and promotes youth acting in productive ways. The institute identified 40 different components and gave the name *Developmental Assets* to these building blocks of healthy youth development. The data consistently show that the power of assets is cumulative: The more assets young people report experiencing, the more apt they are to succeed in school and live positive lives, and the less likely they are to participate in high-risk behaviors such as drug use, violence, and early sexual activity.

The Framework of
40 Developmental Assets® for Adolescents

Search Institute has identified the following building blocks of healthy development that help young people grow up healthy, caring, and responsible.

EXTERNAL ASSETS

Support

1. **Family Support**—Family life provides high levels of love and support.
2. **Positive Family Communication**—Young person and her or his parent(s) communicate positively, and young person is willing to seek advice and counsel from parent(s).
3. **Other Adult Relationships**—Young person receives support from three or more nonparent adults.
4. **Caring Neighborhood**—Young person experiences caring neighbors.
5. **Caring School Climate**—School provides a caring, encouraging environment.
6. **Parent Involvement in Schooling**—Parent(s) are actively involved in helping young person succeed in school.

Empowerment

7. **Community Values Youth**—Young person perceives that adults in the community value youth.
8. **Youth as Resources**—Young people are given useful roles in the community.
9. **Service to Others**—Young person serves in the community one hour or more per week.
10. **Safety**—Young person feels safe at home, at school, and in the neighborhood.

Boundaries and Expectations

11. **Family Boundaries**—Family has clear rules and consequences and monitors the young person's whereabouts.
12. **School Boundaries**—School provides clear rules and consequences.
13. **Neighborhood Boundaries**—Neighbors take responsibility for monitoring young people's behavior.
14. **Adult Role Models**—Parent(s) and other adults model positive, responsible behavior.
15. **Positive Peer Influence**—Young person's best friends model responsible behavior.
16. **High Expectations**—Both parent(s) and teachers encourage the young person to do well.

Constructive Use of Time

17. **Creative Activities**—Young person spends three or more hours per week in lessons or practice in music, theater, or other arts.
18. **Youth Programs**—Young person spends three or more hours per week in sports, clubs, or organizations at school and/or in the community.
19. **Religious Community**—Young person spends one or more hours per week in activities in a religious institution.
20. **Time at Home**—Young person is out with friends "with nothing special to do" two or fewer nights per week.

INTERNAL ASSETS

Commitment to Learning

21. **Achievement Motivation**—Young person is motivated to do well in school.
22. **School Engagement**—Young person is actively engaged in learning.
23. **Homework**—Young person reports doing at least one hour of homework every school day.
24. **Bonding to School**—Young person cares about her or his school.
25. **Reading for Pleasure**—Young person reads for pleasure three or more hours per week.

Positive Values

26. **Caring**—Young person places high value on helping other people.
27. **Equality and Social Justice**—Young person places high value on promoting equality and reducing hunger and poverty.
28. **Integrity**—Young person acts on convictions and stands up for her or his beliefs.
29. **Honesty**—Young person "tells the truth even when it is not easy."
30. **Responsibility**—Young person accepts and takes personal responsibility.
31. **Restraint**—Young person believes it is important not to be sexually active or to use alcohol or other drugs.

Social Competencies

32. **Planning and Decision Making**—Young person knows how to plan ahead and make choices.
33. **Interpersonal Competence**—Young person has empathy, sensitivity, and friendship skills.
34. **Cultural Competence**—Young person has knowledge of and comfort with people of different cultural/racial/ethnic backgrounds.
35. **Resistance Skills**—Young person can resist negative peer pressure and dangerous situations.
36. **Peaceful Conflict Resolution**—Young person seeks to resolve conflict nonviolently.

Positive Identity

37. **Personal Power**—Young person feels he or she has control over "things that happen to me."
38. **Self-Esteem**—Young person reports having a high self-esteem.
39. **Sense of Purpose**—Young person reports that "my life has a purpose."
40. **Positive View of Personal Future**—Young person is optimistic about her or his personal future.

The Power of Assets

On one level, the 40 Developmental Assets® represent common wisdom about the kinds of positive experiences and characteristics that young people need and deserve. But their value extends further. Surveys of more than 2 million young people in grades 6–12 have shown that assets are powerful influences on adolescent behavior. (The numbers below reflect 2003 data from 148,189 young people in 202 communities.) Regardless of the gender, ethnic heritage, economic situation, or geographic location of the youth surveyed, these assets both promote positive behaviors and attitudes and help protect young people from many different problem behaviors.

0–10 assets   11–20 assets   21–30 assets   31–40 assets

Figure 1: **PROMOTING POSITIVE BEHAVIORS AND ATTITUDES**

Search Institute research shows that the more assets students report having, the more likely they are to report the following patterns of thriving behavior:

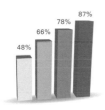 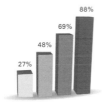 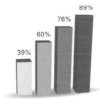 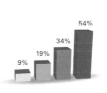

Exhibits Leadership
Has been a leader of an organization or group in the past 12 months.

Maintains Good Health
Takes good care of body (such as eating foods that are healthy and exercising regularly).

Values Diversity
Thinks it is important to get to know people of other racial/ethnic groups.

Succeeds in School
Gets mostly As on report card (an admittedly high standard).

Figure 2: **PROTECTING YOUTH FROM HIGH-RISK BEHAVIORS**

Assets not only promote positive behaviors—they also protect young people. The more assets a young person has, the less likely she is to make harmful or unhealthy choices.

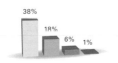 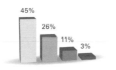 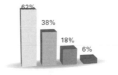 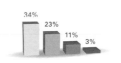

Illicit Drug Use
Used illicit drugs (marijuana, cocaine, LSD, heroin, or amphetamines) three or more times in the past 12 months.

Problem Alcohol Use
Has used alcohol three or more times in the past 30 days or got drunk once or more in the past two weeks.

Violence
Has engaged in three or more acts of fighting, hitting, injuring a person, carrying a weapon, or threatening physical harm in the past 12 months.

Sexual Activity
Has had sexual intercourse three or more times in her or his lifetime.

References

1. Centers for Disease Control and Prevention, "2009 National Youth Risk Behavior Survey Overview," National Center for Chronic Disease Prevention and Health Promotion, 2009. www.cdc.gov/HealthyYouth/yrbs/pdf/us_overview_yrbs.pdf.

2. Jessie Breyer and Ken C. Winters, "Adolescent Brain Development: Implications for Drug Use Prevention." Minneapolis: Center for Substance Abuse Research, Department of Psychiatry, University of Minnesota, & Mentor USA, 2004. www.mentorfoundation.org/pdfs/prevention_perspectives/19.pdf.

3. Substance Abuse and Mental Health Services Administration, "Nonmedical Use of Adderall among Full Time College Students," *NSDUH Report*, April 7, 2009. www.oas.samhsa.gov/2k9/adderall/adderall.htm.

4. J. D. Hawkins, R. F. Catalano, and J. Y. Miller, "Risk and Protective Factors for Alcohol and Other Drug Problems in Adolescence and Early Adulthood: Implications for Substance Abuse Prevention," *Psychological Bulletin* 12, 64–105, 1992.

Chapter 2

Where Do Teens Get Drugs?

THE REALITIES OF SUBSTANCE USE HAVE CHANGED IN TODAY'S WORLD. There are more substances to abuse, and the potency of some illegal drugs has become stronger. The marijuana of today is five times more potent than the cannabis of the 1960s and 1970s.[1] Changes in communication have made it easier to find opportunities to use. It used to be that news of a party that served alcohol was spread by a whisper and a note. Now kids may learn of a party via text, blog, e-mail, or a post on a social networking site—and the news still spreads by whisper and note.

Access is usually what determines which substance takes center stage. Although cigarettes and alcohol are the substances that teens usually use first (because of this they are known as *gateway drugs*), inhalants and prescription medications can also be first substances of abuse because they are present in nearly every household. Over-the-counter cough medicines, diuretics, energy shots, and sleeping pills are sometimes abused for their effects. Even some incense, glass cleaner, and bath salts can be misused to obtain an altered state of mind.

In a 2005 survey by the American Medical Association, two out of three teens reported that it was easy to get alcohol from their homes without their parents knowing about it, and nearly one in four teens reported that their parents had supplied them with alcohol.[2]

It isn't hard to guess where teens get prescription medicines. Statistics show that family medicine cabinets, not street vendors, are the main resource for prescription drugs. Some abused substances, such as over-the-counter medicines and inhalants, are as easy to access as a trip to the grocery or the garage.

Home and Family

A poll of teens aged 13 to 18 found that nearly half reported having obtained alcohol at some point. In all age groups, girls nearly always ranked higher than boys in obtaining alcohol. In the adult poll, about one out of four (26 percent) U.S. parents with children aged 12 to 20 agree that teens should be able to drink at home with their parents present.[3]

Parents who host parties that furnish alcohol can firmly believe they are doing the right thing and being good parents. They reason that teens will drink anyway, and by hosting a party they will keep them safely under supervision. Parents reason that they take car keys from those who drove and provide sleeping arrangements or rides for those who consume alcohol.

Unfortunately, parents don't realize the consequences of their actions. Their attitude teaches that it is okay to break the law when we don't agree with it. It also conveys to teens a belief that alcohol is necessary for social functions. It removes the fear of parental disapproval, which is still a strong inhibitor when it comes to experimentation. The rush of "getting away with" a high-risk behavior is gone too, so teens may be attracted to other negative activities. It deemphasizes the risk and consequences of drinking, and the parent who furnishes alcohol at a party to keep her own child drinking at home also furnishes alcohol to the sons and daughters of other parents who may highly disapprove of the practice.

In addition, eliminating one risk—drunk driving—does not eliminate the other risks associated with alcohol: physical damage, memory loss, fighting or arguing, damaging property, pregnancy, STDs, missed school, and poor performance on school projects. All of these have been noted by youth as consequences of underage drinking.[4]

Parents are not the only trusted adults from whom kids obtain alcohol and other drugs. Any family members over 21 years of age may offer access. This may include siblings, aunts, uncles, and even grandparents. Parents may refuse access to alcohol and be unaware that it's quietly being consumed by their minor children who obtained it from another relative. The reasoning for endorsing substance abuse can be similar to that of the parents' ideas of safety: for example, older siblings may feel that their inexperienced younger brothers or sisters will be safer among family. Sharing this "rite of passage" can be a defining moment in the relationship—and there is sometimes the added bonus of having something to hold over the younger sibling later.

In addition to alcohol, many other substances are available at home. Prescriptions that are not finished by the patient may continue to sit on shelves, along with over-the-counter medicines. Some homes have residents with chronic conditions that require prescription pain medicine or tranquilizers. Teens can easily slip painkillers or depressants from a bottle—and how many of us really keep track of our prescription pill quantity?

Nobody Is Immune

My mother-in-law is a wonderful, trusting person. During Christmas she always has a house full of family, so before the holidays one year, I asked her to hide the oxycodone prescription she takes for arthritis. After Christmas came and went, she noticed that her recently filled prescription for painkillers was missing.

   I asked her later: "What happened? Don't you remember that I told you to hide your prescriptions?" She looked straight at me and replied, "I didn't think you meant family."

Even more readily on hand are household chemicals and aerosols. These can often be the first substances abused because of their availability. Many things that can be inhaled, or "huffed," are found in our own cleaning closets. In March 2010 the Substance Abuse and Mental Health Services Administration (SAMHSA) reported on a new national study that revealed that 12-year-olds are more likely to use potentially deadly inhalants than cigarettes or marijuana.[5]

When our children are young, we put cleaning supplies and solvents up too high for them to reach, and we lock up medicines and block cabinets that contain potential dangers. As responsible adults, we take these precautions to keep curiosity at bay and to keep our children from ingesting things that will hurt them. Their attention is drawn by the colors of the containers or the sound the pills make when the bottle is shaken, instead of by the potential effects of the medication. While that type of curiosity disappears as children grow, peers and the Internet have led to a totally different type of curiosity.

School and Friends

School life makes contact with older kids inevitable. Even time on a school bus ride can grow relationships with older people. A child in grade 6 who had friends in grade 4 is now the adult over 21 years of age with friends who are 18. Today's social networking sites facilitate connections between people at a quick rate, so that friends have friends who have other friends who have other friends. The transitions from elementary to middle school and from middle to high school require every coping skill kids have. It is rare to meet an adult who is willing to go through her teen years again. There is a constant need for a sense of belonging. Popping a tiny white tablet in one's mouth to meet the "dare" seems relatively easy, because the bigger dare is to not fit in at all.

Classmates will provide also. According to the "Monitoring the Future" study, a survey of almost 50,000 teens throughout the United States, there are several ways that teens get their hands on prescription drugs. The most popular method is to take them from home, right from the medicine cabinet. Other methods include getting them from friends, buying them or just asking for them from strangers, and ordering them from illegal Internet pharmacies.[6]

Retail Establishments
. . . .

In a small rural community in the Midwest, youth on probation have said that a primary source of alcohol is the county's large multipurpose retailer. They aren't buying it—they wait until a greeter or security guard is distracted by a security alarm (triggered by an accomplice) and then they take it through the theft detectors. However, stealing is not the only way teens are getting retail establishments to provide alcohol. Another way to get alcohol is the classic "shoulder tapping" technique: a minor will loiter in a liquor store's parking lot, approaching patrons and offering money in exchange for buying alcohol.[7]

Inhalants are readily available in all sorts of aerosols and household chemicals. Though it is not federal law to do so, I have seen some large-scale retailers request that the buyer show proof of age when purchasing airplane glue, canned air, or paint thinners. There is no regulation of aerosol whipped cream and deodorant. All of the above can provide a "trip" for those who inhale the fumes. This substance is extremely easy to purchase and is legal to possess.

Over-the-counter drugs such as cough medicines and sleeping pills are not regulated on a federal level, although the precursors to making methamphetamine are either placed out of direct access or monitored for purchase quantity. Cough medicine is still an easy buy over the counter, as are diet pills, sleeping pills, and stimulants. Again, since there is no regulation on purchase age, younger teens are buying the drugs and taking them for giggles instead of sickness.

However teens obtain substances, it is important to recognize that access *does happen.* The next chapters will provide advice on what we should do when we suspect a teen is using substances, and how to react when a teen comes to us for help.

References

1. National Institute on Drug Abuse, "Research Report Series: Marijuana Abuse," NIH Publication Number 05-3859, Bethesda, MD: NIDA, NIH, DHHS, 2005. www.drugabuse .gov/PDF/RRMarijuana.pdf.

2. American Medical Association, "Adults Most Common Source of Alcohol for Teens, According to Poll of Teens 13–18," *Alcohol Policy MD,* August 8, 2005. www.alcoholpolicymd .com/press_room/Press_releases/adults_give_youth_alcohol.htm.

3. Ibid.

4. Indiana Prevention Resource Center, "Indiana Youth Survey: Annual Monograph," August 2009, www.drugs.indiana.edu.

5. Substance Abuse and Mental Health Services Administration, *The NSDUH Report: Trends in Adolescent Inhalant Use: 2002 to 2007.* Rockville, MD: SAMHSA, 2009.

6. L. D. Johnston, P. M. O'Malley, J. G. Bachman, and J. E. Schulenberg, *Monitoring the Future: National Survey Results on Drug Use, 1975–2008: Volume I, Secondary School Students* (NIH Publication No. 09-7402), Bethesda, MD: National Institute on Drug Abuse, 2009.

7. R. Gassman, M. K. Jun, S. Samuel, et al., *Alcohol, Tobacco, and Other Drug Use by Indiana Children and Adolescents: The Indiana Prevention Resource Center Survey—2010* (IDAP Monograph No. 10-01). Bloomington: Indiana Prevention Resource Center, 2010.

Section II

Prevention, Intervention, and Treatment

Chapter 3

Prevention Strategies, Policies, and Practices

I TURNED ON THE TELEVISION ONE NIGHT AND STARTED TO WATCH A movie that featured a woman in rehab for methamphetamine use. Not really wanting to watch a movie about substances, I changed the channel to the Judy Garland movie *A Star Is Born*. I turned to it just in time to watch her cry over her husband's alcohol addiction, lies, and constant promises to do better. Changing the channel once more, I landed on a well-known series that my daughter watches. The main character is obnoxious, angry—a steady drug abuser who stays on the fringe between unemployment and rehab. He is the hero of the series.

There are many mixed messages about substance use in our society. Markers have fruit smells, even though we are not supposed to inhale the fumes. Proms feature shot glasses and wine glasses as prizes, even though students are not old enough to drink. Media of all types portray substance use as "no big deal": alcohol distributors and distilleries sponsor Internet games; beer commercials play during sports games; movies portray substance use as a neutral or even positive choice; and television shows use drinking to enhance drama. The people in alcohol advertisements are most often beautiful and young looking, situated in very desirable, happy scenarios. All these examples of use provide a feeling of familiarity, making substance use seem comfortable and approachable.

In 2007, 75 percent of students used alcohol before graduating, according to the Youth Risk Behavior Surveillance System. Nearly 4 out of every 10 students had used marijuana. The average age for the first drink of alcohol is under 13.[1] These numbers are overwhelming, and no after-the-fact interventions will appreciably reduce them. Our hope and first response must be prevention.

Community Education and Awareness

Substance abuse is a community issue. Rates of substance abuse will not change until our environment does not accept illegal substance use as normal. When vast majorities of youth are using legal and illegal substances for entertainment prior to graduation, it is not just a parent issue or a school problem. Statistics show that those who use alcohol prior to age 16 are very likely to have addiction issues later. Also, younger teens who have become devoted fans of alcohol are more likely to experiment with other substances.

It affects us all. We'd like to think that people stay in their homes to abuse marijuana. That they never drive unless they are sober. That they never miss work, never leave the house too high to function, and never use health insurance or public assistance due to their addiction. Society as a whole would like to think that individual substance abuse is not a community issue. But it *is* a community issue.

Drug use is associated with other high-risk behaviors such as unprotected sex, vandalism, assault, and domestic violence. Various drugs cause long-term chronic health problems such as heart disease, lung disease, brain damage, liver and other organ failure, and cancer, which put a strain on community resources. Community impacts stem from the association of drug use with motor vehicle crashes, suicide, homicide, drowning, boating deaths, rape, assault, and robbery.

Current analyses of the costs generated by drug use problems in the U.S. population estimate that the U.S. economy absorbed $70.3 billion in alcohol costs and $44.1 billion in drug abuse costs. Most of the costs of drug abuse are due to crime. Associated costs include police protection, public legal defense, property destruction, and productivity losses for those who engage in drug-related crime. There are costs involved for people incarcerated as a result of a drug-related crime. Additionally, researchers have linked substance use during high school and young adulthood to lower educational attainment and lower earnings.[2]

Substance abuse often comes to the attention of a community in one of two ways. First there is a report of increasing abuse of a single drug, such as meth or heroin—perhaps from law enforcement and hospitals. It becomes the focus of community interest, federal attention, and counterdrug measures. Actions are put into place to fight the problems associated with the substance, and gradually the abuse of that particular drug declines. But as this drug of choice declines in use, another rises to take its place. The real issue is not a specific drug, but rather the people who are driven to seek it out. Users are still users. The substance of choice is different, but the problem of substance abuse hasn't changed. That is why in many cities arrest rates for one type of drug may drop even as those for another increase.

Substance abuse can also become a community issue when a personal tragedy occurs. Most of us can recall stories of a promising youth who died at the hands of a drunk driver, or of a kid who drove under the influence and permanently changed the course of his life through an accident. This seemingly isolated event did not affect only the driver and the victim. It affected their families, the newspaper that reported the event, the religious community that prayed for their families, the friends who mourned with the families, the law enforcement officers and emergency medical technicians who responded to the accident . . . the list goes on.

Both of the above scenarios show a pattern of being reactive instead of proactive. Although reports of drug trends and personal tragedies are sometimes jumping-off points for public awareness campaigns, they are still after the fact. They are reactive. Being proactive would have involved using prevention efforts to stop the substance abuse and subsequent burden on society in the first place. Efforts are needed to change the environments that surround areas of the community that lend themselves to drug arrests. These efforts cost money, true, but treatment programs, court trials, and prisons cost even more.

Visible law enforcement and an active judicial follow-through on arrests are key opportunities to effect change in a community's substance abuse troubles. When others see that a person has broken the law, or broken school rules, and has been disciplined as a result, it creates a stronger inhibition among everyone else. The key is to be open and available about the process, so that people know that there are true consequences to their actions. And making the process more transparent may also hold the judicial system or school administration more accountable for following through on their policies.

Other items, such as a change in policy and stricter laws at the community level, can help curtail underage drinking and drug rates. Policies are a big opportunity to impact an entire community. This starts with educating the officials who govern the changes. We cannot anticipate making any alterations until those who have the power are well informed.

Policies can be as bold as an ordinance that makes hosting a party allowing underage drinking a criminal offense, or as simple as an order that instills a curfew or limits access to retail alcohol sales. Fairs and festivals that sell alcohol can be required to train their servers and even set limits on alcohol accessibility.

Communities can establish a system that rewards retail establishments that refuse to sell to minors. They can create certificates and door signs that advertise their status as law-abiding stores, and promote them in local newspapers and on websites as retailers that support the community's youth.

Efforts can also include neighborhood revitalization. Areas with high drug arrest rates can be improved by sponsoring physical cleanup days, installing additional lighting, and neutralizing hidden areas where drug transactions are completed. Neighborhood councils can provide alternative activities for families that change perceptions of family values and lower other negative statistics. Since our schools are often centrally located in a neighborhood, they can be a prime setting for social outreach and services.

Adult Education and Awareness

After 50 years of warnings and education, we are finally seeing a possible decline in tobacco use. After about 40 years or so of campaigns and legislation, seatbelt usage has increased. Education and awareness are our chief tools in making changes in tobacco, alcohol, and other drug use among teens and, in turn, among adults.

It is in our best interest to educate parents and other adults to the real issues of substance abuse. How many would be shocked to learn that about three-quarters of teens will have consumed alcohol for entertainment by the time they graduate from high school? Would it disturb them to know that nail polish remover and aerosol deodorants have recreational purposes?

Educating and bringing awareness to adults about an issue does not have to come in large, heavy-handed graphs of data and statistics. Small, purposeful, and continual information is more effective. When shared in a continuous and ongoing manner, what was once a long, dull education piece can become a series of small digestible bites that have a better chance of being retained.

There are many creative ways in which we can draw parents onto the prevention path. Some schools promote a "parent pledge." The pledge is a promise that when teens are in their homes, parents will provide positive alcohol-free and drug-free supervision. This may enlighten parents to the reality of risky behaviors and encourage them to think about where their own children are spending time.

Events, public speakers, and short-term prevention celebrations help increase awareness of substance abuse among adults and youth—that is, when they are used as part of a larger plan to lower drinking and drug use rates. Otherwise they are effective for only a short period of time. Think of it this way: a student poised in front of a beer with friends is not likely to remember the words of a public speaker from three months ago. But as a component of a comprehensive approach that includes additional proven prevention methods, one-time events can help bring the message home that alcohol and drugs should not be part of a young person's life. There are many types of evidence-based programs and environmental projects designed to educate and bring awareness that use such events as components, but include other methods as well to help continue to educate.

Realistic Expectations

We must not assume that all parents who sign such a pledge are serious. Some parents will simply sign a pledge because it looks good on paper. Teens know which homes have parents who supervise and which homes have parents who are clueless. Kids who want to drink and abuse other drugs will migrate to houses where parents aren't home or are not monitoring their activities. Some parents and even grandparents abuse substances alongside their children or grandchildren. Students still know where to go to get the alcohol, prescriptions, and illegal drugs.

As students, we learned new math equations and formulas each year. We were usually taught to first go back to the basics of addition, subtraction, multiplication, and division and then add new material. So it is with a comprehensive drug prevention project. To be effective, the messages for prevention should be continuous and ongoing throughout each year of a young person's school career. The messages should be brought home and into the adult community as ongoing and usable information on substance abuse prevention.

Our children are educated at a young age about substances. Prevention is taught in school and use is taught in social settings. Adults are a massive resource for prevention that remains virtually untouched when it comes to teen drug use. A large portion of the adult population has been misinformed or not informed at all about the truths of substance abuse. "It's a rite of passage" or "There's nothing we can do about it" are common responses from an uninformed adult population. At an adult community level, through education and awareness approaches, we can take action to provide prevention efforts. Lack of knowledge is an enemy. Ignorance is not bliss. Misinformation about teens and substance abuse can cause adults to do more harm than good.

We would do well to have trainings and in-services for those who spend time with teens. In the day-to-day struggle of grades, schedules, and pressing school issues, an educator's radar has not been set to scope out alcohol or drug use. Parts of any job become second nature, but substance abuse does not walk into the office every day. We need to be armed to watch for it and deal with it as if it were common.

Many schools have a zero-tolerance policy for tobacco, alcohol, and other drug use—some even extend beyond school boundaries. It's usually called upon to provide punishment (or help) for students who are known to have abused substances. But there is no policy, procedure, or protocol to use in the event that a student is *suspected* of substance abuse. Ideally, there should be a set of rules to address such situations and offer guidance for those on the front lines.

Schools could provide a procedure for teachers who suspect a student needs substance abuse help, counseling, and/or treatment. It could establish a route of communication for those who need to be in the loop concerning the student. Before the student even becomes party to the conversation, other teachers, other school personnel who have influence, coaches, counselors, and administrators could be informed. Each of them could add a new perspective and provide necessary information to take additional steps. Even if their observations don't add up to a conclusive decision about whether or not a teen is abusing drugs or alcohol, members of this team would be "on alert" and take extra time to monitor the youth.

By educating our adult population to the signs and symptoms of substance abuse, we are giving information to the people who may be the first line of defense against this enormous problem. By educating them to the potential damages, we are better preparing them to help a teen make decisions about substance use. Teens are very well informed about their drugs of choice; adults should be also. Showing youth that we know what is going on can prevent use in the same way that telling the public about extra police patrols on Memorial Day weekend deters drunk driving. Better-prepared adults weave a web of protection and prevention.

Teen Education and Awareness

Youth are taught from a very young age to "Just Say No," and a lot of schools participate in a weeklong celebration that focuses on staying drug free. But these messages, in and of themselves, have not been shown to be effective in fighting substance abuse.

Antidrug campaigns that are not backed by a continuous message lose their force and are forgotten very quickly after the event. For the same reason, flyers and other printed materials have little effect on most individuals. Leaflets are most likely part of a landfill soon after they are handed out. Seldom do you hear that a single speaker, a flyer, or a ribbon was the deciding moment for an individual to not do drugs. More often the reason is a combination of many different factors that provide a teen with the power to refuse substances, including positive relationships with adults, involvement in activities, and strong connections to parents or guardians.

While "Just Say No" is simple, it is of little use when the next prompt in the conversation is "Why not?" or "We won't be friends if you don't." Teens faced with refusing drugs are not doing so in a conversation with a seedy-looking drug dealer, where they can run away after the invitation. A more comprehensive, evidence-based program is required. Evidence-based programs have lessons that are geared to teach teens and younger youth what to say *after* "No." These programs are designed to help students not only understand the problems associated with recreational use of substances but also learn cognitive skills, social skills, and self-efficacy. The Substance Abuse and Mental Health Services Administration (SAMHSA) keeps an up-to-date National Registry of Evidence-Based Programs and Practices that lists over 160 intervention programs, each of them carefully evaluated for reliability and effectiveness (www.nrepp.samhsa.gov). They have been proved successful in various settings, populations, grade levels, and genders, and the search engine at SAMHSA's website allows you to sort through programs based on specific criteria to suit individual needs.

Practicing the Response

One of my girls had a horrible school bus situation. The assigned seat put her with a few students who took pleasure in her reactions to their teasing. Every day, she came home distraught from her bus ride. I offered to call and have her seat switched, but she said that wouldn't solve the problem. So we began to work on how to retaliate when the aggressors began to bother her.

From experience, I knew that ignoring bullying in the hopes that it will go away is about as effective as ignoring an infection and hoping it will cure itself. She and I talked about the things the other students said and how they approached her, and we worked on different responses, manners, and body language. This helped on several different levels. We were doing something proactive to help her fix her own dilemma, which gave her confidence. I showed her that I knew her situation was hard and that I wanted to help her solve it. She learned how to handle an aggressive circumstance, which helped her later in life when faced with similar situations. And the bullying students eventually gave up and left her alone.

Risk and Protective Factors

Risk and protective factors play serious roles in a teen's ability to turn down the offer of substances. Many risk factors are outside our scope of abilities to change. However, by knowing that certain lifestyles and behaviors are precursors to substance abuse, we can narrow the field of teens practicing high-risk behaviors. Two researchers from the University of Washington, J. David Hawkins and Richard F. Catalano, have spent more than 20 years researching risk and protective factors that contribute to drug abuse. They are divided into specific areas of influence:

INDIVIDUAL/PEER

Risk Factors

- Alienation and rebelliousness
- Friends who engage in the problem behavior
- Favorable attitudes toward the problem behavior
- Early initiation of the problem behavior

Protective Factors

- Belief in generalized expectations, norms, and values of society
- Skills to successfully take advantage of meaningful opportunities to contribute to the community
- Positive temperament
- Religiosity
- Prosocial ability

FAMILY

Risk Factors

- Family history of high-risk behavior
- Family management problems
- Family conflict
- Parental attitudes and involvement in the problem behavior

Protective Factors

- Strong external support system
- Strong parental bonding
- Strong family interaction
- Parent-youth discussion about drugs and alcohol use

SCHOOL

Risk Factors

- Early and persistent antisocial behavior
- Academic failure beginning in elementary school
- Low commitment to school

Protective Factors

- Strong commitment to school
- Alcohol and drug education curriculum
- School-related activities such as sports, student government, music, drama, and other prosocial involvement

COMMUNITY

Risk Factors

- Availability of drugs
- Community laws and norms favorable toward drug use
- Transition and mobility
- Low neighborhood attachment and community disorganization
- Extreme economic and social deprivation

Protective Factors

- Bonding to a community that promotes healthy beliefs and clear standards
- Involvement in faith community activities
- Involvement in after-school activities
- Meaningful opportunities to contribute to the community
- Reward, recognition, and acknowledgment of efforts[3]

There are risk factors that we will not be able to control, such as a "family history of high-risk behaviors" and "economic deprivation." By the time a teen reaches middle school, the chance to alter "academic failure in elementary school" is long gone. On the other hand, many of the protective factors can still be emphasized, such as "meaningful opportunities to contribute to the community" and "reward, recognition, and acknowledgment of efforts." It is never too late to strengthen certain protective factors, and doing so may keep a young person from intensifying his or her substance abuse or from experimenting with drugs in the first place.

References

1. Centers for Disease Control and Prevention, "2009 National Youth Risk Behavior Survey Overview," National Center for Chronic Disease Prevention and Health Promotion, 2009. www.cdc.gov/HealthyYouth/yrbs/pdf/us_overview_yrbs.pdf.

2. Lisa Werthamer and Pinka Chatterji, *Prevention Intervention Cost-Effectiveness and Cost Benefit Literature Review*. Bethesda, MD: National Institute of Drug Abuse, 2008.

3. M. W. Arthur, J. D. Hawkins, J. A. Pollard, R. F. Catalano, and A. J. Baglioni Jr., "Measuring Risk and Protective Factors for Substance Use, Delinquency, and Other Adolescent Problem Behaviors," *Evaluation Review* 26, no.6 (2002): 575–601.

Chapter 4

Early Intervention

PRACTICAL EARLY INTERVENTION INCLUDES DEFINING THE NEEDS OF the child. In our circumstances it happens, hopefully, *before* the need for treatment. This is where our expertise as members of his or her life has power. He may be a casual user, not yet at the point where addiction counseling is needed. She may have more fear and guilt than an actual drug problem. Early intervention opportunities manifest primarily with those students who, with proper help, can walk away from possible long-term effects or drug dependence. With early intervention and quick action, we can head off large consequences such as expulsion or legal action, and perhaps prevent a true drug addiction from taking hold. It is when teens are past the point of experimentation that adults are past the point of preventing substance abuse.

Dealing with substance abuse is not a simple, linear path. When a student asks for a schedule or class change, we can answer yes or no. When a student needs help with a relationship, asking the right questions can clarify the logical next step, which we can suggest. If a student has problems with a class, we can suggest a tutor or set up help during study hall. Those students are often in and out in a quick single movement: problem solved and case closed. But a substance abuse issue is an ongoing project. It requires our full attention: involving other adults, seeking additional help, and monitoring progress

Keep in mind, too, that a teen seeking help is not necessarily the one abusing substances. She may be the daughter of someone addicted to prescription painkillers. He may be the brother of someone who can't quit smoking marijuana. The issue may be a friend's experimentation with illegal drugs or inhalants. In this case, the person who has the drug issue is not sitting in the office and hasn't come asking for help. It may be tempting to reach out to the person who is actually abusing substances, but we can only help someone who *wants* to adjust her situation. We can, however, work in the background, keeping a watchful eye on the person in question and building additional protective factors.

When You Don't Know What to Say

Unfamiliar situations can leave us at a loss for words. The best way to start finding those words is to get as much information as possible. This needs to be a time of clearheaded questions that will help us assess the situation correctly. The priorities are to listen, assure the teen that he is being understood, and take his concerns seriously.

So when we don't know what to say, we listen. We build a relationship as well as an accurate picture of the high-risk behavior. Such questions as "Can you explain how that happened?" and "How long ago was this?" tell the student that we're paying attention and help us gather as much information as possible. Rather than focusing on the behavior of the past or dreaming of a long-term goal in the future, we listen to where the teen is at this precise moment. Then, with the teen in control, we slowly construct plans to address the immediate situation as well as the high-risk influences he's experiencing.

When a Young Person Admits Involvement with Drugs

The old adage about "How do you eat an elephant?" applies here: just take it one bite at a time. If a teen comes to you voluntarily about a substance problem, then it stands to reason that she has at least some openness to adjusting her behavior. The steps to making any change start with modifying how we think, feel, and act. Start small.

We don't need to develop a list of big things that have to be corrected immediately, such as low grades and poor attendance, at the first meeting. Important as those things may be, the student's overall lifestyle choices are more important. The strategy here is to look for a small easy "win"—something that can build up the student's sense of accomplishment. It should be something that *we* can build upon as well. Drugs are comfortable and desirable, but a sense of accomplishment and positive feedback can be desirable, too. We can plan this win with the teen; in fact, it is best if the student picks the challenge. We gather all the information we can and then we work with the teen to set one short-term obtainable goal or step—one small bite.

Reality Check

Be prepared for the reality that a student may visit you once and never come back. Her reasons for showing up in the first place can be complex: Perhaps she received ultimatums from her parents. Perhaps she is failing school or has lost a job. Maybe she has had a run-in with the authorities. Sometimes a visit to a teacher or youth group leader can be a delaying tactic or the only alternative to an "or else" situation. Unfortunately, the simple fact that she has a substance abuse problem means she has deceived countless people before you, and may also be deceiving *you*. Our human desire to care for small puppies and crying babies may kick in, and we can get lost in the role of super-teacher, super–youth leader, or super-counselor, but we must keep our feet firmly on the floor and put our cape back in its box, because the teen has a very long journey ahead of her.

There is no set rule about what a teen should work toward first. First steps are individual to each teen's circumstances, which is why it is necessary to get the full story and have the student's buy-in to the process. The point is to have the teen break away from the pattern and get used to a different activity, thought process, or feeling. Once the goal is set, we must hold her feet to the fire: she should be accountable for the basic goal without excuses.

However, it is our responsibility to be certain this goal is easily obtainable. We can guide by limiting the number of choices: "Well, all those sound great, but let's start with one decision: should you do X, or Y?" This is a salesman's tool. By giving a choice between just a few things, we are limiting the teen's chances of saying no.

Learn from her. What are her normal patterns of activities? A small change here might seem inconsequential, but it could shift the dynamics of an entire day and cause a ripple effect. Talk about:

- being in places where adults don't provide or allow alcohol and drug use
- staying in public when she hangs out with friends
- applying for a job—not *getting* a job (that's a mammoth bite), but just getting the application, filling it out, and returning it to the employer

- rekindling a friendship with someone who doesn't use substances (try to get a name from the student)
- going to an all-ages concert or event where drugs will not be present (try to identify a specific event)

Notice that these goals are tactile and observable. By providing a doable task, the goal has a beginning, middle, and end. It offers a quick opportunity for a sense of accomplishment. As we learn more about the teen, goals will shift in many directions, and we may find that some types of goals are more effective than others: some teens work better with goals that deal with feelings and thoughts, while others prefer outwardly directed actions. The main thing is to keep the goals small, specific, and achievable.

Though being off substances, making passing grades, and staying in school are important priorities, they are not the first steps on the road to sobriety. Steps further along the way will include those. Particularly in the beginning, tasks should be chosen based on their chance of success. This helps both us and our student. It helps us gauge a youth's sincerity and commitment to change by seeing whether or not she completes an easily manageable task. And by ignoring the really big stuff for the time being and setting a safe goal, the youth can feel that her overwhelming load has gotten lighter. She will believe that your concern goes beyond the walls of the school. There will be a better chance for a lasting effect when the goal is based on restructuring thinking, feelings, and actions. In addition, one success can lead to another. Putting together successes outside drug use can build up a student who wants to become clean and stay clean. As these actions begin to multiply, it will show in other behaviors. As actions and thinking change, so do feelings. Planning for another meeting after the goal is achieved lets the teen know there will be accountability and helps her understand how seriously we take the problem.

In the background, contact other adults in the student's life. It isn't necessary to share the dirty details; just ask for feedback about her, about recent changes. We are verifying the truthfulness of the student and weaving a web of adult relationships and support. These will be eyes and ears to provide feedback as well as suggestions.

As small changes bring new beginnings, they may bring negative consequences. Friends may not like new attitudes or their associate's newfound success. Family may question her change. When we involve other adults, they may find that keeping an extra eye on the student is a nuisance. Be prepared for setbacks. Be prepared to see the teen return to drug use. Be ready for that sheepish grin, the shoulder shrug, and the dismissal that lumps us in with all other adults. The student's reason for seeking us out may have changed, or the power of the drugs and her friends may be stronger than her desire and ability to be clean. Our time and energy are not wasted. We have left the teen with tools that may promote sobriety later. We have left the teen an open door to return and start again (and again, and again). We have been left to ponder whether we need to intervene further through treatment or counseling.

Putting It in Perspective

Start a pro and con list with the teen. It can be updated and maintained throughout the process. In this case, the goal could be to add a certain number of items to each side of the list. It seems simple enough for the teen to list what is "good" about continuing to abuse drugs: there are positives such as friends, self-image, and the body's reaction to the substance. But here is where our knowledge of the side effects, short- and long-term effects, and physical and psychological damage can help with the negatives. Putting extra emphasis on the negative physical, visible side effects will speak to a teen's ego. We can express why her current habits could lead to a very destructive end, but not in prison or in car wrecks while driving under the influence, because these are intangible possibilities to our seemingly "immortal" teens. Instead, we can focus on what commonly happens to a youth who uses substances, including the visible negative effects such as hair loss, tooth decay, and weight gain or loss, and the tangible loss of trust, relationships, and education that are more immediate to a teen than a vague "someday" they don't really believe in yet.

When a Young Person Won't Admit Involvement with Drugs

Other reasons besides the actual drug abuse may provoke a teen to seek assistance. The side effects of use may have started to take their toll. He may find other parts of his life in jeopardy. When working with a teen who shows the signs and effects of substance use but refuses to admit use, we are treading on eggshells. The teen may not provide any assistance to change his situation. He is not the willing subject.

Dealing successfully with the user who doesn't want or believe he needs to be clean may seem—or even be—impossible. The best approach is to focus on the specific reason for his visit and build from the cause of the meeting by addressing the issue that brought him there. Grades, attitudes, absences, behavior, or even a simple discussion about classes can be a starting point. We must be certain the goal or step we agree on meets the needs of the problem, is attainable, and brings a sense of accomplishment. Perhaps the goal will be to guide him through making up a seemingly insurmountable amount of overdue class work, one assignment at a time. Perhaps the goal is for him to use alternative behavior when a situation does not suit him. Keep things simple: change will not happen until enough things occur to make him *want* to be clean.

Our best opportunities may come later in the student's life, as we leave the door open for future discussions. We can let the teen know we are available and work toward having follow-up meetings about the problem at hand. If we really listen to his story he will know we understand. The best approach is to provide a caring school climate, opportunities for engagement with after-school and school-based opportunities, positive adult role models, and a safe environment.

When Someone Else Is Abusing Drugs

Sometimes kids come to see us because they're worried about other people—maybe a friend, sibling, or parent. Such a student will probably be very concerned and upset. Here, too, we need to listen carefully. The substance abuser may be "just" experimenting—or the abuse may have brought their relationship to a complete halt. The student may have misconceptions about substance abuse that range from heavy-handed scare tactics to myths told by other students. We need to make sure we know the whole story.

In rare cases, the drug user may be a danger to the student. At this point, decisions need to be made with the help of outside authorities. Information that a student is in danger *must* be shared; keeping such information from the proper authorities is unethical and puts the student at risk. Before beginning to discuss a situation, it is important that we let the student know that danger to himself or others will change the privacy level of the conversation.

When a Young Person Says a Friend Is on Drugs

When a student comes to us to say she fears a friend is using drugs, our priorities here must be with her and not the friend. It may be tempting to try to reach out directly to the friend in question, but again, we can't help someone who isn't willing to be helped. If the student does give enough detail that we can identify the student who is abusing drugs, then we can quietly work in the background to help that person as well, using some of the tactics that were outlined in the previous section, but that may be as far as we can go on our own.

For now, we need to focus on the student in front of us. Fear, ignorance, intimidation, worry, and uncertainty have driven her to seek advice. While her friend's condition is *her* worry, her mental health and well-being have got to be *our* main concern. As she works to help the friend, we need to be mindful that she is getting good and positive social interaction from other venues. This substance-abusing friend should not be her only focus; healthy relationships with other teens will be necessary. The problem friend may choose not to become clean, which could devastate our student. Without other relationships, she may feel isolation, failure, and loneliness.

In addition, the teen needs adult support. There are so many ways in which we cannot (and should not) be her only source of adult confidence. Encouraging her to talk to her parents will help ensure that she does not fall prey to drug use herself. It brings a sense of accountability and can boost positive family communication. Parents can also encourage other relationships or activities to help balance the child's current circumstances.

The idea of talking to her parents may be met with some resistance, so it will be helpful for us to walk through the consequences of telling or not telling (a pro and con list may be useful here). Including parents may help her think about talking to the friend's caregivers and how best to approach the situation. It would be risky, on many levels, for her to report drug abuse to the friend's guardians without the support and encouragement of her parents. It is a layer of extra protection from those who know her best and are consistently part of her world.

This should not be a one-time talk. It's a good idea to plan a follow-up discussion to be certain she is getting the help she needs.

When a Young Person Says a Sibling Is on Drugs

When someone comes in saying he thinks a sibling is abusing substances, we generally follow the same procedures as when a friend is on drugs—but with the added twist that we have to carefully consider family dynamics. The whole story in this case will be more complicated. The sibling may no longer be living at home, or may be in treatment or incarcerated. He or she may have mental health issues. The parents may or may not be aware of the matter. The sibling may have been abusing for a long time, but now the student is ready to face the situation. The sibling could be much younger or much older. Each situation calls for a different approach. Listening to the student is still our starting place. We have to work from his perspective in order to help him.

Through questions and the complete story, we can begin to find the root of the issue. While we don't have to be as mindful about a quick win, we do have to instill that same sense of accomplishment. Since the student is not the user, we can set goals that are more than one-time, easy accomplishments.

A concern that may cross the student's mind is his own susceptibility to addiction. While addiction does have a genetic link, environment plays a significant role as well. When parents and other adults are careful to model the proper use of substances, then generational use has far less opportunity to take control. Other influences can also significantly reduce the chance for habitual substance use, including clean, positive friends, good social interactions, resilience skills, and involvement in school-based activities.

If we discuss the idea of involving his parents and he is reluctant to do so, we should explore the reasons why: it will give us another layer of information to work with. If there is no imminent danger to the student, calling parents is not our option—but affording him the choice to work as a team with his parents *is* an option.

When a Young Person Says a Parent Is on Drugs

Parents are an unmatchable resource of love and compassion, so children don't usually attach blame to the parent for the drug use. Instead there is fear for their future and worry for the parent's health and safety.

Children whose parents are abusing alcohol or other drugs sometimes assume that most other moms and dads do also, and they don't see it as a situation that requires help. Or, children may be acutely aware of how their parents are different, and are embarrassed or afraid to admit it. In addition, kids may be reluctant to ask for assistance because they fear being removed from their families. No matter how bad life at home may be, it is still difficult for anyone to trade a known situation for an unknown one. Young people know that by confiding in adults, they risk being taken away from everything that is familiar and possibly being separated from their siblings. These things make a child who has lived within the walls of regular and constant drug addiction his entire life very unlikely to ask for help.

Not as Seen on TV

It's hard not to picture dramatic images of a meth lab or a parent whose forearms are riddled with needle marks. But there's a good chance that that particular student will not be standing in your office asking for help. It's not that such students don't need help—it's that they either have already been removed from the situation or believe the world they have had all their life is normal.

When a young person does come to us for help, we should proceed carefully and slowly. We should try to develop a full picture of the situation through conversation and interaction. Her parent or guardian may be dependent on painkillers or smoke marijuana or be an alcoholic. And sometimes what a child perceives as abuse really isn't: she may believe that drinking a glass of wine with dinner could be an issue because it is daily use. Again, it's important to listen and carefully construct the real story so we can create an action plan.

In some cases, the student will need to talk with other people, such as a social worker. Cases that involve the authorities will affect family life, school, friendships, and other activities. Our role here is to support the teen. We can provide guidance so that the life changes she must incur are as few as possible.

We can help the teen identify strengths in her behaviors, thoughts, and feelings that she can draw upon. We should ask questions about eating and sleeping habits to be certain that her health is not an issue. We should keep an eye on her, and, if possible, other adults should know that this teen is experiencing some tremendous stress—but proceed carefully. Since this is a sensitive issue, relaying specific information to others about what the teen is dealing with may do more harm than good. In addition, the protocol to follow may be predetermined in some cases, and our involvement may be limited by the authorities.

Chapter 5

Seeking Help

WHEN A YOUNG PERSON COMES TO US SEEKING HELP WITH SUBSTANCE abuse issues, it's important to bring in reinforcements. We need to get adults on board who are important to the student, whether they are parents or guardians, teachers or staff, or other adults with strong connections to the student. The young person's individual situation will determine whom we contact, and it's important to explain to him that we will be connecting with other adults, so that he won't see it as a breach of trust or "tattling." If possible, we should work with the student to choose the adults we are going to contact. Some situations, however, will require us to contact the local authorities; reports of physical or sexual abuse, or the commission of a crime, generally must be reported to officials as soon as we learn of them. Individual "mandated reporting" guidelines vary by state and province, so it is important to be aware of them.

Talking with Parents and Caregivers

When talking with parents, guardians, or caregivers, we have to walk a fine line when it comes to how much "advice" we can give. It's not enough to say, "your child needs to see the family physician," and hand Dad a leaflet on substance abuse, but it's also wrong to start the conversation with, "I think your son is on drugs."

It is very easy to make all sorts of assumptions about the parents of a drug abuser, but the situation the student is in might not be based on his home life at all. We should not approach a conversation with parents or caregivers with the presumption that their lifestyles are responsible for the teen's behavior. The student may live in an environment where substance abuse is a natural phenomenon—or his parents may be shocked and horrified by the very mention of it.

We shouldn't anticipate a specific reaction, either. Some parents don't have negative feelings about alcohol or other substance use. Or we may run into cultural misunderstandings. In some societies, the consumption of alcohol and illicit smokeable substances is an expected part of family tradition. If we insist that it is wrong, we run the risk that we will alienate ourselves from the family and create additional difficulties. Before we call, we need to make sure we understand the situation as thoroughly as possible, from all the angles. We also need to be aware that the teen himself may not be entirely truthful about his family life: he may give us an inaccurate description as a way to help support his excuses for his negative behaviors.

When we do call, we should call early on in the situation. This shows the parent that we are not keeping secrets. We aren't doing the student any favors by trying to let him "solve it himself," or by working on the problem without a parent's help.

When we telephone, we should first make sure it is a good time to talk, then make sure we don't rush in. Let's start with what we know: facts that we have seen and things we can prove. For instance, "Your son's grades have been slipping," "I have noticed that he is not participating in basketball," or "A teacher has removed him from class for falling asleep" may be good conversation starters. We should then allow the parent to expand on this. Parents have different ideas about how much information they want concerning their child's negative behaviors, and some prefer to remain uninformed. If the parent gives no response, we can ask if they have seen changes in behavior at home.

Though research and statistics say that such changes in behavior are most likely related to drug use, other circumstances could be the root of the problem. It's a good idea to inquire whether there have been any outside factors that could have influenced his actions. Ask about behaviors outside school that are signs of concern, such as not being at home, changes in eating and sleeping habits, or a lack of communication. As the conversation continues, the parent may speak of notable signs such as unusual smells on the teen or in the car, frequent use of air deodorizers, or unique containers, wrappers, and paraphernalia.

Parents and guardians may be reluctant to accept a substance abuse problem. They may be busy, stressed, anxious, or distracted. They may be resistant, convinced that they know best. They may want to ignore the issue and assume it will go away. Whatever the case, our position is to be certain that parents and guardians know this call isn't without reasonable provocation, that we will be working with them for a solution, and there is support from other adults who spend time with their child.

When we make the phone call we are not just informing parents of a problem. We are opening a Pandora's box of social stigma. Attitudes that surround the parents of teen substance abusers can be shaming and cold. Their child's drug use is not news easily shared with friends, coworkers, or even family. Not only does it shake their faith in their ability to parent, it causes a reframing of their interactions in society. So while your side of the conversation may be a calm, even gentle statement of facts, such as "Your child is skipping school . . . We've noticed a slip in his grades . . . These are sometimes signs that indicate drug use . . . ," parents and guardians are reacting much more emotionally, thinking things such as:

- My child may die from doing something stupid.
- My child has an issue that may never go away or may permanently damage him.
- I messed up.
- Things will never be right again.
- All the things I hoped for him are in jeopardy.
- This can't be fixed with duct tape.
- I can't tell anyone because they will think I am a bad parent.
- How will he recover his grades?
- Now what?

With a few exceptions, kids using substances do not have parents smoking dope and dropping acid in the living room. Nor does a mother look into the face of her newborn child and whisper, "Oh, there's my little high school dropout and marijuana addict." We need to emphasize to parents and guardians that it's not a predestined curse to be the caregiver of a teen who abuses substances. The more that parents, the teen, and other adults see eye-to-eye and work together on getting him clean, the better his chances are of staying clean. We can emphasize that this imperfect child has made a series of bad choices and now the problem needs to be corrected. Drugs may have changed not only grades, reputation, and friendships but also attitude, mood, and thought patterns. Since drugs take control of our thinking, feeling, and actions, the return to a sense of normalcy is a very long trip. The familiar normal may never return. This parent may be facing an early intervention that turns around quickly, or a very lengthy recovery—similar to the recovery from a physical accident. The same sympathy and kindness extended in the case of an accident need to be extended here.

Unfortunately, there is no script for this kind of conversation. We are back to plain conversation—not from authority to parent, but from concerned team player to parent. We need to show support and make a plan that falls in line with the plans we've made with the teen. We should set a time to "check in" so the parent knows there will be future opportunities to talk, and to encourage accountability on the part of the parent. Then we must keep the promise and call for updates.

Talking with Other Adults

Teens take their relationships with their teachers personally. How many times have we heard, "That teacher doesn't like me"? That statement indicates just how much influence a teacher can have over a student. We may be met with resistance when asking teachers to pay particular attention to a student, especially when that student is not a "shining star" in class. There is more satisfaction when designing time around those who want to learn rather than those who just want to sleep. Classroom teachers have to juggle standards for teaching, curriculum needs, and the best interests of the general student population all at the same time. When we add the need to keep a special eye on a student who doesn't necessarily look like she can be "saved" anyway, teachers aren't always enthusiastic partners in the process.

Caring Works

I was met with resistance while trying to help a freshman student with behavioral issues. André's teachers were all too willing to hand the boy over to me so he would no longer interrupt the classroom. He was a large kid who was prone to moodiness and lacked motivation. I was told his older brothers were in jail and the teachers were certain he was headed there, too.

André spent a year with me before both he and I were sent to separate school systems. I met him again about six or seven years later. I was having a particularly stressful day and had walked into a grocery store for a few last-minute items. A man in his early 20s, working behind the deli counter, gave me an enormous smile and asked if I had been his counselor. After all those years, he had remembered me. He had so many things to brag about. He graduated from high school and holds a steady full-time job at a place I know demands ethics and accountability. He is the very proud father of an eight-month-old baby.

A well-meaning or resistant adult needs to be brought into the action plan with a specific responsibility. In general, we get far more volunteers to work when we can identify individual tasks. The role each adult plays in the child's life will help to decide his role in the intervention process. A favorite teacher may have more luck with an inquisitive conversation. Coaches can provide a different perspective on a teen's motivations and behaviors. Different adults with different relationships can be very effective.

Those adults who are reluctant to be part of the team may still be able to help. They may respond better to picking their own task. We can help facilitate this by giving them options, such as watching for changes in behavior patterns, keeping notes on class events (both negative and positive), or saying something positive and appropriate whenever there is an opportunity. Team members who keep logs of the progress or regress can help identify patterns and suggest new steps in the process.

When to Seek Outside Help

A teen is not on a desert island: he has a vast number of adults and other associates in his life. We should *always* seek outside help. Outside help can be other teachers and adults who are a part of the teen's early intervention team. Outside help can be counselors or other colleagues who serve as sounding boards for ideas and next steps. Outside help can be a parent. Outside help may have to be social services or an authority if there is a threat of harm to the teen or someone else. And, except in the case of social services, it's not always necessary to share the specific details of a situation, since it's important to preserve the dignity of the student and family.

When a student comes to us for help, we can talk through plans, encourage her to talk with parents, and start gathering a group of concerned adults, but our level of intervention should stop at the office door. Unless or until we receive specific training for personal intervention in drug abuse cases, it isn't ethical (or sometimes even safe) to go any further than that. And when other agencies and authorities are called upon, we must limit our involvement according to policy and protocol. That doesn't mean we are giving up on our student, just that there needs to be one authority in the matter to avoid sending her mixed messages.

When to Contact a Social Worker

By law, there are times that we are required to seek the assistance of social services. When a child is under a threat of harm, action must be taken to protect him. However, the decision to call social services should be made with approval and advice from our administrative superiors. We should never fly solo when it comes to the health and well-being of the children: we do not do them any favors by keeping their issues a secret. No matter how the teen perceives our interference and influence, our first and foremost duty is to protect him. Requirements for reporting substance use vary by state and province, so we must make sure we are up to date on the latest rules.

When to Call Law Enforcement

We are not in the "business of kids" to be coldhearted, but our compassion and feelings for the child cannot be given precedence over the law. Our laws exist to protect us as a society. When we involve law enforcement, it states many positive things. For instance, it sends a message that certain behaviors are not tolerable. It states that the police are a good resource for troubled youth. We are not abandoning the teen— we are protecting her from causing irreversible harm to herself and hurting innocent people. If we don't follow the legal system properly, we have reduced our ability to help. By not following the law, we would be sending the message that it is okay to bend the rules. We are trying to bring these children back to a sober, clean lifestyle, preferably without a police record. However, sweeping illegal actions under the rug and providing her an opportunity to repeat the offense could have possibly devastating consequences.

Ideally, our school, religious community, or youth program will have policies and protocols in place to avoid personal judgment calls regarding issues of illegal use, chronic use, or knowledge of intended use. We need to be familiar with these policies and protocols, and if our workplace doesn't have them, we should spearhead a movement to create them.

Chapter 6

....

Kids and Treatment

....

TREATMENT MAY NOT BE IN OUR CORNER OF THE WORLD, BUT IT IS IN the adjacent neighborhood. Treatment may be the necessary control mechanism to clean and detoxify a teen, and it can provide assistance far beyond our capabilities. It provides safe physician care and can address additional problems such as mental illness, suicide, guilt, and anxiety. It can address the aftereffects of drug use such as weight loss, flashbacks, and cravings. Treatment has the ability to provide a combination of psychiatric care and medication to help control habitual drug abuse.

We are not qualified to do what inpatient and outpatient treatment services provide. Our limited ability to help ends when there is chronic use, and treatment is the answer when our efforts have not changed the situation. When drugs are destructive to the abuser, or dangerous thoughts and actions such as harming himself or someone else are present, it calls for treatment.

There can be a stigma to substance abuse counseling because it falls under the umbrella of mental health, but chronic, habitual substance abuse and addiction are not a "pull-yourself-up-by-the-bootstraps" situation. Emphasize to the student and others involved that seeking external help for mental health is no different from seeking assistance for a physical need. Substance use changes the way our brains operate and our bodies work. Reversing the effects can be very difficult, and it may be unattainable without trained professionals.

A good example is tobacco use. The addictive ingredient is nicotine, which affects the brain so that it craves the results from the drug. We all know people who keep smoking even though they know the negative side effects, even when it begins to affect their physical health. People continue to smoke even though they know that quitting will reverse most of the negative side effects of use. And we all know people who have desperately tried to quit using tobacco and have failed. Products that help people quit smoking are a multi-million-dollar business.

Nonsmokers are very willing to accept the idea of smoking as an addiction. Otherwise, the practice makes little sense. Why else would someone want to inhale dried leaves (and who knows what else), heat, and paper into his lungs? Why would someone want to alienate herself from society by being forced into the few areas of the community that permit smoking? Why would people continue to do damage to their own bodies, smell like an ashtray, potentially hurt the people around them, and spend money to do it? The answer is simple: they're addicted.

People accept nicotine use as an addiction and encourage smokers and those who chew tobacco to join programs that will help to stop the chronic use. The same should apply to any addictive substance. The basic need for help is the same.

Kids Who Are in Treatment

Treatment can be medication, counseling, group therapy, mental health outpatient care and inpatient hospital care, mental health programming, or a combination of all of these. Inpatient care is used most often when possible dangers have entered the picture, including attempted suicide, violent behavior, overdose, abuse, threat of personal harm, chronic use and addiction, or when other methods have proved ineffective.

A teen in treatment is getting the psychological help he needs to improve his circumstances. As members of his support group, we can continue to support him outside his mental health care. Taking an interest in him and being a safe and reliable resource outside treatment are appropriate. However, it is not in the teen's best interest for us to play an active role in his therapy. Continue the healthy net of teachers, family, and other adults.

If inpatient treatment is necessary for a teen, he often has the chance to maintain his schoolwork during his hospitalization. We can be the liaison for such a situation, connecting all the dots between the school, teachers, and health-care service providers. If deemed suitable, we can encourage the student through appropriate channels such as mail or phone. Upon the student's return, we can continue to monitor grades and other progress to avoid additional pressure or a repeat of stressful scenarios.

Kids Who Have Completed Treatment

. . . .

Medicines that treat addiction are most effective when used with a therapy program. There are types of medication that treat specific addictions. In some cases, treatment may be an ongoing process. A student may begin with an intense treatment plan and eventually graduate to intermittent, "as needed" therapy or group therapy programs. These kids have newfound behavior skills and cognitive thinking skills.

Treatment and Medication

Treatment may involve the use of medications, which can cause several types of changes: the teen may have a period of adjustment to the drugs that mimics signs of substance abuse; antianxiety medication will cause sleepiness and lethargy; stimulants may change eating patterns and cause excitability. In most cases, antidepressants are not advised for kids under 18 years of age as they may cause suicidal tendencies. Drug treatment therapy may take weeks to become a properly working tool. There are times that a teen will need to try different medications to find the one that will suit her brain's chemical balance best.

A teen who has been hospitalized has been separated from her friends and peers. Her return will hopefully come with fanfare and enthusiasm. However, she will return to the same community and environment she left. The only person who has changed in these circumstances is the teen. As a young person, it is very easy to sink back into the same habits and temptations that caused the hospitalization in the first place. Good therapy extends long beyond the release from inpatient care to prevent relapse. Our assistance through observation of progress can be valuable. The parents and therapists will need information on changes in temperament, behavior, grades, and attendance. Our involvement helps to round out the mix of adults in her life who will hold her accountable for putting her new mental health skills into action.

After teens return from therapy, our position returns to monitoring grades, attendance, and discipline. Changes in these can signal a need to provide information to parents. We help through supporting them and maintaining an approachable attitude.

When treatment ends, the teen may wish to return to a life that does not include extra visits with adults. With a broken bone, we all look forward to the day the cast comes off and the doctor releases us to return to normal activity. So it goes with mental health. The doctor has released the teen to return to normal activity. Providing an environment without kid gloves and special treatment will promote experiences and events that will prepare her for the real world where, outside of family, friends, and an adult support system, there will be no one who will give her special handling.

Kids Who Have Relapsed

Relapse is common. Treatment centers can consider it part of the treatment process. When teens are in the safety of treatment, they are monitored and aware of the factors that initiated and prolonged their substance use. However, most treatment plans will end. Teens will return to the same home, school, stress, classes, and friends. The teen may even come back with a false sense of control and security because he has become clean, learned new coping skills, and lived in sobriety for the term of his treatment.

They may have the knowledge and may know the skills to fight returning to drugs, but in the midst of old familiar friends and places, keeping the commitment to stay clean is difficult. Some will fight relapse for their entire life.

Our best defense against this is to help the teen have people he can call upon without judgment. We developed the web of adults to mentor and observe the teen when substance abuse first reared its ugly head. When the teen stops treatment, the web continues—perhaps not in as much depth as before, but to monitor behaviors and actions. Should something such as attitude or attendance begin to change for the worse, the team is on alert, ready to start the battle all over again if necessary.

We go back to small steps with guaranteed successes; we go for the win. We return to having regular meetings to monitor progress and hold the teen accountable. We recognize the importance of involving him and his parents. We have to again look at outside factors to discern whether other things could be causing the change in behavior, such as his medications, or whether he has indeed relapsed.

If a student relapses, this doesn't mean he, or we, have failed and have to go all the way back to square one. This is a kid we know can succeed without drugs. It will be easier to get the web of adults together this time because they have seen the clean teen. It will be easier to talk with parents and guardians because we have an established relationship. It will be easier to work with the teen because he knows what is expected of him and he knows he needs help.

Section III

What Are Teens Abusing?

Chapter 7

Over-the-Counter Substances

THERE ARE MORE THAN 100,000 OVER-THE-COUNTER (OTC) MEDICATIONS, divided into more than 80 categories. Teens use a variety of OTC medications for entertainment. Depressants, stimulants, and hallucinogens are available off the shelves of any pharmacy, and teens who are willing to swallow the right amount will do so to achieve the desired effects. Under normal circumstances, over-the-counter drugs can be used without a prescription and without a doctor's supervision so long as they are taken according to the manufacturer's directions. When searching for a high, however, kids and teens don't follow those directions, and severe consequences can result.

While our children are little, we lock up the over-the-counter medicines and we obey the "Keep Out of Reach of Children" warnings on household cleaners and chemicals. When we do, we help keep our young children safe. Until they understand the dangers in swallowing chemicals and medicines, it is our responsibility to provide them with a secure environment.

Once our children get older, it still needs to be impressed upon them that the warnings surrounding medicines and other household products apply at this age too. It's hard for teens to realize that cough medicines given to a toddler and aerosol-canned whipped cream are products associated with death and brain damage.

Dextromethorphan

The cough suppressant dextromethorphan (DXM) is found in over-the-counter cough and cold medications. The effects from DXM abuse can be as significant as hallucinations and out-of-body experiences, depending on the amount ingested. DXM is found in syrups (such as children's cough medicine), tablets (such as adult cough medication), gel capsules, lozenges, and strips that melt in the mouth. It is also available as a prescription powder. As with all OTC medications, if it is taken as directed, it is generally safe. However, the rate of poison control center phone calls that involve DXM abuse is on the rise.[1]

DXM is one of the most commonly abused over-the-counter medicines, with 5.5 percent of students in grade 12 reporting use in the last year.[2] When it is abused for entertainment, as little as two ounces can compare to a high from illegal hallucinogens. DXM abuse has developed into a disturbing trend. In May 2009, the Food and Drug Administration said in a paper warning against DXM abuse, "Today's teens are more likely to abuse Rx and OTC medications than . . . illegal drugs like Ecstasy, cocaine, crack and meth. Nearly one in five teens (19 percent or 4.5 million) report abusing . . . prescription and over-the-counter drugs."[3]

Dextromethorphan is an opiate agent. It has similar effects to the use of morphine or LSD (see Chapter 8). The effects of DXM differ according to the amount consumed: a low dose (as little as about 200 milligrams of pure dextromethorphan) causes euphoria; a middle-sized dose initiates vivid imagination and closed-eye hallucinations; a high dose (about 600 milligrams) sets off alterations of consciousness and out-of-body experiences.

Short-term effects of DXM abuse include double vision, dry mouth, and stomach pain. The real danger of DXM abuse comes from overdosing on the other ingredients in cough medicines as well, such as acetaminophen. Those side effects include nausea and vomiting, organ damage, and infertility. Signs of DXM abuse include confusion and lethargy, redness of skin, and slurred speech.

Dextromethorphan Fast Facts

 Other names for dextromethorphan include DMX, De-De, Tussin, Triple C or CCC, Purple Drank, Dex, Poor Man's X.

 Short-term use of dextromethorphan can result in double or blurred vision, dry mouth, and abdominal pain. Nausea and vomiting are effects due to the amount of cough medicine someone would have to ingest to get a reaction. Irregular heartbeat, loss of movement, dizziness, and loss of motor control can occur.

 Long-term use of dextromethorphan can result in organ damage and infertility.

 Signs associated with dextromethorphan use include confusion, seizures, and lethargy. Effects on appearance and speech include dry itchy skin, slurred speech, redness of the face, and sweating.

Stimulants

When used properly, stimulants help restore mental alertness or wakefulness. They are also used as appetite suppressants. Over-the-counter stimulants mimic prescription stimulants, but contain lower doses, and active ingredients include ephedrine, pseudoephedrine, and caffeine. After the Combat Methamphetamine Epidemic Act of 2005 was passed, products containing ephedrine and pseudoephedrine became more heavily regulated in the United States, and are now kept behind the pharmacy counter and sold in limited amounts.

Types of stimulants include over-the-counter appetite suppressants, decongestants, caffeine pills, and energy drinks—most of which are abused for the very effect they are designed to produce. Teens may think that because these products are legal, they are less dangerous than other drugs. They see caffeine, in particular, as harmless because of its prevalence. But consuming caffeine in coffee or soda is very different from taking caffeine in a pill: it's very difficult to consume overdose-level amounts of caffeine by drinking coffee, and much easier to overdose in pill form.

Because national surveys to date have combined questions about OTC and prescription stimulants, data on only over-the-counter abuse of stimulants are unavailable. Many of the same effects of abuse that are found with stimulant and depressant prescription drugs are found with their OTC counterparts. While they are safe at the recommended dosage, it is dangerous to use these chemicals in excess. Short-term effects of stimulant use include dizziness and tremors, wakefulness, hyperactivity, and reduced appetite. Long-term use can cause a fast heartbeat and chest pain. Signs of stimulant abuse include weight loss, restlessness, panic, agitation, and insomnia.

Stimulant Fast Facts

 Some over-the-counter stimulants include NoDoz, Vivarin, caffeine pills, Monster Energy, Red Bull.

 Short-term use of stimulants can result in dizziness and tremors. People using stimulants may also feel a reduced appetite, extremely awake, and hyperactive.

 Long-term use of stimulants can cause an unusually fast heartbeat, chest pain, and tremors.

 Signs associated with stimulant abuse can include being underweight and experiencing physical tremors. Effects on behaviors include restlessness, confusion, panic, inability to concentrate, insomnia, and agitation.

Inhalants

. . . .

Inhalants restrict the amount of oxygen provided to the brain while substituting certain other chemicals. Basically, while adding a chemical into the brain, inhalants also rob the body of oxygen, creating a short-lived high. A reaction from inhalant abuse does not last very long, so users may continue to huff to maintain the high. Some products of choice include spray glue, correction fluid, markers, gasoline, vegetable oil sprays, spray paint, and nail polish remover.

Inhaling or "huffing" the fumes from rags soaked in cleaners and chemicals is one method for abuse. Another method is spraying the chemical into a bag and inhaling from the bag. Inhalants are sometimes the drug of choice because they do not show up on drug screens. Teens who are in a program that demands a drug test will use inhalants to continue their drug use. Inhalants can be far more dangerous than the chemicals that do show up on urine test strips. The results are more unpredictable and their use is not measured in pill or syrup form.

Studies show that students in grade 8 experience the highest level of inhalant abuse, with 8.9 percent reporting abusing inhalants in the past year, which makes it the most-abused type of substance among middle school children. Numbers among students in grades 10 and 12 are lower, at 5.9 percent and 3.8 percent, respectively. Inhalant abuse overall, though, appears to have been trending downward in the last decade.[4]

Short-term side effects of inhalant abuse are similar to alcohol use: dizziness, lack of coordination, and confusion. Long-term effects include delusions, weight loss, muscle weakness, irritability, and depression. Signs of inhalant abuse include red or raw skin around the mouth and nose, similar to a sunburn, sniffles, slurred speech, weight loss, and a chemical smell on the breath or clothing.

Inhalant Fast Facts

 Names for inhalants or inhalant use include moon gas, huffing, laughing gas (nitrous oxide), snappers (amyl nitrite), poppers (amyl nitrite and butyl nitrite), whippits or whippets (fluorinated hydrocarbons, found in whipped cream dispensers), bold (nitrites), and rush (nitrites).

 Short-tcrm usc of inhalants rcsults in symptoms similar to alcohol use, such as dizziness, lack of coordination, lightheadedness, confusion, and delirium. After-effects include a headache and drowsiness. Loss of consciousness may occur after repeated use over a short period of time.

Long-term use of inhalants can induce delusions. It can also result in weight loss, lack of coordination, and depression.

Signs associated with inhalant abuse are varied, and include raw, red skin around the mouth and nose similar to a sunburn, sniffles, slurred speech, weight loss, chemical smell on the breath or clothes, disorientation, and lethargy.

Sleep Aids and Antihistamines (Depressants)

Sleep aids and allergy medicines are sometimes based on the same antihistamines, called diphenhydramine hydrochloride and brompheniramine maleate. Taken as instructed, the medication will relieve mild sinus issues and cause drowsiness. Taking more than the amount needed to relieve allergies or insomnia can cause anxiety, tremors, and restlessness. There are no current statistics on how many kids and teens abuse antihistamines or sleep aids.

Laxatives

Laxative abuse occurs as attempts are made to rid the body of unwanted calories by using purgatives. They can be a diet additive and are sometimes linked to someone who suffers from an illness called bulimia nervosa. A person with bulimia nervosa overeats (binges) and quickly rids his body of the food through various methods (purges). The rationale is that by taking laxatives, the body will not absorb the calories and the food will become waste. This methodology is faulty, and a diet containing frequent laxative use will cause malnutrition. Laxative abuse is serious and dangerous.

Though the issue is still addiction, the body becomes dependent in a different way. Tolerance can develop, and the user needs to take more laxatives in order for them to perform the same function in the intestines. There are many negative physical effects from prolonged laxative abuse. Laxatives as well as diuretics (water displacement pills) can cause the levels of sodium, potassium, and magnesium to change. Electrolytes and minerals necessary for normal body functions, such as the use of nerves and muscles, can be affected. The colon and heart can be permanently affected. Laxatives can cause severe dehydration, which can be indicated by a headache (as in a hangover), tremors, blurry vision, and weakness. The national rates of laxative abuse among kids and teens are unknown.

Pain Relievers

The three most common over-the-counter pain relievers are aspirin, acetaminophen (Tylenol), and ibuprofen (Advil and Motrin). All three products work well to control minor headaches, muscle aches, menstrual cramps, arthritis pain, and fever.

Doctors even recommend small daily doses of aspirin for people with heart trouble. That particular blood-thinning quality used to help those with heart problems can be the very component that causes damage when overdose occurs.

Pain relievers are rarely abused for entertainment. People who deliberately take too much of a pain reliever are usually attempting suicide. In emergency room visits of those under 21 years of age, overdoses of pain relievers have shown a rise in numbers from 2004 to 2008.[5]

Dietary Supplements

Dietary supplements are a growing business. While most supplements are helpful, mixing them with other medications can cause serious consequences. Most labels on dietary supplements don't spell out drug interaction issues, but the combination of OTC medications or prescription medication with supplements can have adverse effects.

Supplements are found in bars as extracts or concentrates. They also come in tablets, capsules, soft gels, gel caps, liquids, or powders. Abuse of dietary supplements is uncommon among kids and teens; abuse that does occur mainly involves performance-enhancing supplements and tends to happen for the same reasons that teens abuse anabolic steroids. Common performance-enhancing supplements include caffeine, creatine, protein, beta-hydroxy-beta-methylbutyrate (HMB), and ephedrine and ephedra (ma huang).

Caffeine, as discussed earlier, is a common performance-enhancing ingredient in energy drinks, power bars, and the like. It has been shown to increase endurance and improve concentration. Negative effects increase with higher dosages, however, and can lead to increased heart rate, dehydration, irritability, and insomnia.

Creatine is a popular supplement intended to build muscle mass and improve reaction times, particularly in sports that require "explosive power," such as football, wrestling, and baseball. Creatine use has been associated with asthmatic symptoms, weight gain, stomach discomfort, heat intolerance, and electrolyte imbalances leading to seizures.

Protein in the form of powders and shakes are also popular among kids and teens trying to add muscle mass. The normal North American diet, however, contains enough protein to fuel most athletic activities, and even athletes in the midst of intense training do not need much more than that. Too much protein in the body can result in kidney problems and dehydration.

HMB, taken in pill form, is intended to improve the body's oxygen efficiency, increase muscle mass, and decrease body fat. Only a few short-term studies of this supplement have been conducted, so long-term side effects are unknown.

Ephedrine and ephedra, also discussed earlier, are supposed to burn fat, boost metabolism, and increase endurance. Side effects include anxiety, high blood pressure, hallucinations, and seizures. Its use has been banned by many sports organizations

References

1. National Drug Intelligence Center, "Intelligence Bulletin: DXM (Dextromethorphan), Document ID: 2004-L0424-029, October 2004.

2. L. D. Johnston, P. M. O'Malley, J. G. Bachman, and J. E. Schulenberg, *Monitoring the Future: National Survey Results on Drug Use, 1975–2008: Volume I, Secondary School Students* (NIH Publication No. 09-7402), Bethesda, MD: National Institute on Drug Abuse, 2009.

3. Partnership for a Drug Free America, "DXM Abuse Warning," May 15, 2006.

4. Johnston et al., *Monitoring the Future*.

5. Drug Abuse Warning Network, "2008: Selected Tables of National Estimates of Drug-Related Emergency Department Visits," Rockville, MD: Office of Applied Studies, SAMHSA, 2009.

Chapter 8

Restricted Legal Substances

SOME SUBSTANCES ARE LEGAL BUT AVAILABLE FOR PURCHASE ONLY under certain restrictions, while others can be obtained only with a doctor's prescription. Laws restricting the purchase of alcohol vary by state and province, as do laws governing the purchase of tobacco products. Governments across the world have also sorted drugs into "schedules" (with some variations by country) based on their potency and potential for addiction, ranging from Schedule I, which lists drugs unavailable even by prescription, such as heroin, to Schedule V, which includes substances that are considered "low risk" for addiction but still require a doctor's prescription, such as cough suppressants containing small amounts of codeine.

Nicotine/Tobacco

Because nicotine use (in the form of cigarettes, cigars, snuff, chewing tobacco, and pipe tobacco) is legal, there is a perception that it is less dangerous than other drugs. But nicotine and tobacco use should not be dismissed so easily: it is highly addictive, it is the cause of one-third of all cancers, and it is the most common drug abused by youth today, with nearly a third of all students in grade 12 reporting that they've used tobacco in some form within the last month.[1]

Nicotine is an alkaloid stimulant found in tobacco plants. When tobacco is smoked, it produces a very short-lived high—a quick burst of euphoria and faster heart and breathing rate that are followed by a steep drop. This is why smokers experience a feeling of calm when they use cigarettes: what they are really feeling is the mild "crash" after the initial high.

Tobacco production, purchasing, and advertising are regulated by governments, and the minimum age to purchase tobacco products in the United States is 18. Cigarettes are the most popular way to consume tobacco, and they contain over 4,000 additives, some 400 of which are known poisons, including tar, formaldehyde, cyanide, and ammonia.[2]

Short-term effects of tobacco use are coughing and irritation of the lungs (when smoked), and yellowed teeth and fingernails. Long-term effects include various types of cancer, depending on the type of tobacco used. Cigarette smoking can cause lung cancer, emphysema, and chronic bronchitis, and it increases the risk of heart disease; using smokeless tobacco increases the risk of many oral cancers. "Secondhand smoke"—the term for exhaled cigarette smoke and smoke given off by burning tobacco products—also presents long-term health risks, including an increased risk for heart disease and respiratory problems in nonsmokers, and accounts for approximately 38,000 deaths per year, according to the Centers for Disease Control.[3]

Signs of tobacco use vary according to the type of tobacco. Those who use cigarettes can smell of smoke, have a cough, experience frequent respiratory illnesses, and have yellowed teeth and nails. Those who use smokeless tobacco can have yellowed teeth and spots on the gums and tongue.

Nicotine Fast Facts

✓ **Nicotine is found in** cigarettes, cigars, smokeless tobacco (chewing tobacco, snuff, snus, gutka), shisha (smoked in a hookah), dokha (smoked in a midwakh), and in smoking cessation products such as nicotine gum, the nicotine patch and inhaler, and nicotine nasal spray.

✓ **Short-term use of nicotine** can cause an irritated cough in smokers, and stained teeth and fingernails for both smokers and users of smokeless tobacco. Nicotine use leads to a faster heartbeat, higher blood pressure, quickened breathing, and higher blood sugar.

✓ **Long-term use of nicotine** can lead to various health problems. Smoking causes lung, larynx, mouth, kidney, stomach, and bladder cancers, among others, and is directly linked to strokes, heart disease, and emphysema. Smokeless tobacco users face an increased risk of cancers of the tongue and cheeks, gum disease, and a possible increased risk of heart disease.

✓ **Signs associated with nicotine abuse** are yellow teeth, a dry cough, the smell of tobacco, and frequent respiratory illnesses. Signs of smokeless tobacco use include yellow teeth and dark spots on the gums and tongue, and a bottle, can, or other "spittoon" is necessary when using smokeless tobacco.

Alcohol

Alcohol is a depressant. It is produced by the fermentation of yeast, starches, and sugars, and is the intoxicating ingredient in beers, wines, and liquors. References to alcohol have been found in the hieroglyphics in ancient Egyptian tombs, and the discovery of Neolithic beer jugs suggest humans have been brewing alcohol since the Stone Age.[4]

The United States and Canada have had an uneasy relationship with alcohol, with both countries going so far as to completely prohibit it: individual Canadian provinces passed (and later repealed) prohibition laws at various times between 1900 and 1930, and the United States enacted a complete federal ban on alcohol for more than a decade, beginning in 1920. Today, the production and sale of alcohol are carefully regulated.

The 2009 Youth Risk Behavior survey found that 42 percent of high school students reported consuming alcohol in the past 30 days, and that 24 percent reported binge drinking. (Binge drinking is defined as four drinks for a female at an individual sitting and five drinks for a male.) The same survey reported that 10 percent of students reported driving after drinking alcohol, and 28 percent reported riding in a vehicle with a driver who had been drinking.[5]

As the previous statistics show, drunk driving is a major concern when it comes to youth and alcohol. The current legal driving limit for blood alcohol content (BAC) in all states and Canada is a minimum of .08, although many states and provinces have "zero tolerance" laws for underage drinking and driving. It is easier to get to an illegal blood alcohol content than one might think. The intoxication effects are relative to food in the stomach, tolerance level, weight of the drinker, duration of time, and gender. On average, to cause a .02 blood alcohol content level in a 150-pound person, it takes 12 ounces of beer, 5 ounces of wine, or 1.5 ounces of hard liquor within a one-hour period.

Alcohol has a tolerance level that needs to be continually raised to get the same results or level of inebriation. But the drinker's BAC does not decrease with an increase in tolerance. Thus, a heavy and chronic drinker who consumes 36 ounces of beer may show fewer signs of inebriation than an infrequent user who consumes 36 ounces of beer. However, they will both show the same amount of alcohol in the bloodstream.

Alcohol does not stay in the system for a long period of time. The side effects of use can be anything from a slight light-headedness to death, depending on the amount of alcohol consumed and the size and tolerance of the person consuming it. Short-term alcohol use causes dizziness, dehydration, slurred speech, difficulty processing external stimuli, and slowed reaction times. Long-term alcohol use can cause memory loss, addiction issues, weight gain, and blood pressure problems. Heavy drinking can increase the risk of brain and nerve damage, ulcers, high blood pressure, heart disease, stroke, certain cancers, and liver disease.

Alcohol Fast Facts

 Alcohol can be found in different amounts in products such as beer, wine, liquor, ale, cider, and "hard lemonade."

 Short-term use of alcohol can result in slurred speech, dizziness, lack of coordination, confusion, delirium, nausea, vomiting, and loss of consciousness. Drinking too much alcohol in a short time can cause alcohol poisoning, which causes vomiting, seizures, slow or irregular breathing, and low body temperature, and may lead to death. Aftereffects of alcohol consumption include headache, dehydration, and nausea.

 Long-term use of alcohol can cause memory loss, addiction issues, weight gain, and blood pressure problems. Heavy drinking can increase the user's risk of nutritional deficiencies, weight issues, brain and nerve damage, ulcers, high blood pressure, heart disease, stroke, certain cancers, and liver disease.

Signs associated with alcohol abuse include slurred speech, poor coordination, and the scent of alcohol on breath and clothing. Additionally, schoolwork and other activities are not the central focus and will suffer as drinking becomes a priority. Lethargy and sleeping more than normal can also indicate alcohol use. If the liver is being affected, the user may show a yellow (jaundice) cast to the skin. Broken facial capillaries (giving the appearance of a red nose and/or cheeks) may also appear.

Prescription Drugs

. . . .

There are more than 10,000 prescription products in the United States, consisting of approximately 1,500 different drugs. There are 20 to 50 new medications approved each year. And, usually, when we use prescription drugs according to our doctor's directions, they cure our illness and we feel better. However, proper use of certain prescription drugs can lead to dependence, and improper use is becoming increasingly common. The most commonly abused drug categories are stimulants, central nervous system (CNS) depressants, and opiates. Athletes abuse prescription anabolic steroids for their performance-enhancing effects rather than for recreation.

The Internet has become one of the major ways people obtain prescription drugs—and it is becoming increasingly easy to obtain them illegally. As of May 2010, there were 6,469 Internet drug outlets, of which approximately 83 percent do not require a valid prescription for drug purchases.[6]

The Schedule of Controlled Substances

Drugs in the United States are broken down in categories, or schedules, based on their potential for addiction. The schedule ranges from those drugs that are illegal for use (Schedule I) to those that are legal and have small addiction potential (Schedule V).[1]

Schedule I

(A) The drug or other substance has a high potential for abuse.

(B) The drug or other substance has no currently accepted medical use in treatment in the United States.

(C) There is a lack of accepted safety for use of the drug or other substance under medical supervision.

Examples include GHB, heroin, LSD, and mescaline.

Schedule II

(A) The drug or other substance has a high potential for abuse.

(B) The drug or other substance has a currently accepted medical use in treatment in the United States or a currently accepted medical use with severe restrictions.

(C) Abuse of the drug or other substances may lead to severe psychological or physical dependence.

Examples include cocaine (used as a topical anesthetic), oxycodone, morphine, Dilaudid, Dexedrine, and codeine.

Schedule III

(A) The drug or other substance has a lesser potential for abuse than the drugs or other substances in Schedules I and II.

(B) The drug or other substance has a currently accepted medical use in treatment in the United States.

(C) Abuse of the drug or other substance may lead to moderate or low physical dependence or high psychological dependence.

Examples include anabolic steroids, ketamine, and Vicodin.

Schedule IV

(A) The drug or other substance has a low potential for abuse relative to the drugs or other substances in Schedule III.

(B) The drug or other substance has a currently accepted medical use in treatment in the United States.

(C) Abuse of the drug or other substance may lead to limited physical dependence or psychological dependence relative to the drugs or other substances in Schedule III.

Examples include Xanax, Ambien, Valium, and phenobarbitol.

Schedule V

(A) The drug or other substance has a low potential for abuse relative to the drugs or other substances in Schedule IV.

(B) The drug or other substance has a currently accepted medical use in treatment in the United States.

(C) Abuse of the drug or other substance may lead to limited physical dependence or psychological dependence relative to the drugs or other substances in Schedule IV.

Examples include cough suppressants that contain small amounts of codeine, Lyrica, and antidiarrheals that contain small amounts of opium.

———

1. Summarized from *Schedules of Controlled Substances, U.S. Code*, vol. 21, sec. 812 (2009).

Stimulants

Stimulants are also known as *uppers*. They have uses that treat disorders as varied as congestion, narcolepsy, and attention deficit hyperactivity disorder (ADHD). As a prescription, they are most commonly taken orally. An abuser may snort or inject them.

Amphetamines are the dominant form of stimulant. They are usually classified as a Schedule II drug. They are manufactured or synthesized. In the 1930s, amphetamine was first marketed as Benzedrine, which was an over-the-counter inhaler to treat congestion. Dextroamphetamine (trade name Dexedrine) and methamphetamine (trade name Methedrine) were readily available during World War II to keep U.S. troops in a mental state for combat. Of course, this meant that use and abuse from addiction went up after the war was over. In the 1950s, the United States dispensed amphetamines to troops in Korea. In the 1960s, amphetamines became a tool for weight control and a way for truckers to complete their long routes without falling asleep. It was used to help athletes perform better and train longer and was considered a treatment for mild depression.

Different surveys show that in 2008 the annual prevalence of amphetamine use among high school students decreased significantly from the mid-1990s. The 2008 Monitoring the Future survey indicated that 10.5 percent of students in grade 12 had used amphetamines in their lifetime. We must be careful to note that the survey precludes that students know the formal name of the substance in question. For instance, the question "What amphetamines have you taken during the last year without a doctor's orders?" assumes that the survey taker knows what he took at a social gathering was indeed an amphetamine. These students may know them better by brand name or slang.[7]

Short-term side effects of stimulants include dizziness, tremors, impaired speech, and numbness. Long-term side effects include fever, tremors, high blood pressure, and antisocial behavior. Long-term use can also create a psychological dependence. Signs of stimulant abuse can include dilated pupils, sweating, and runny nose. Behaviors include restlessness, inability to concentrate, agitation, and mood swings.

Stimulant Fast Facts

 Stimulants include Benzedrine, Desoxyn, Methedrine, Adderall, Dexedrine, Concerta, nicotine, and amphetamines. Slang terms include *speed, whizz,* and *black dex.*

Short-term use of stimulants can cause dizziness, tremors, impaired speech, and numbness. People using stimulants may also experience a reduced appetite or insomnia, and be hyperactive. Headache and blurred vision may also be present. The abuser may see positive effects such as creative or philosophical thinking, improved confidence and self-esteem, and a sense of increased energy and exhilaration. Stimulants can cause an increase in alertness, concentration, and physical endurance.

Long-term use of stimulants can result in a psychological dependence. Higher doses result in fever, an unusually fast heartbeat, chest pain, blurred vision, tics, tremors, and antisocial behavior. Someone who is using stimulants may have psychological side effects such as agitation, aggression, hostility, and panic. Chronic use may result in dry and itchy skin and convulsions, a strong sense of paranoia, and hallucinations. Suicidal or homicidal tendencies can also be part of stimulant side effects. Abuse can mimic schizophrenia, such as delusions, hallucinations, disordered thinking, and a sensation of distance from one's environment.

Signs associated with stimulant abuse can include dilated pupils, rapid respiration, profuse sweating, runny nose, and being underweight. Other signs include sores, a flushed face, mouth and gum problems, uncontrollable movements or shaking, facial itching, and needle marks. Behaviors include restlessness, confusion, panic, an inability to concentrate, and being secretive. Other strong behavior changes can include agitation or defensiveness, uncontrolled movement or shaking, frequent absences, isolation and withdrawal, and mood swings.

Central Nervous System Depressants

Central nervous system (CNS) depressants, also known as downers, sedatives, and tranquilizers, are used to treat anxiety, panic attacks, and sleep disorders.

CNS depressants vary in effectiveness due to their strength and speed of reaction time in the body. The CNS depressants known as barbiturates produce a wide variety of reactions, which range from mild sedation to coma. They have been used as sedatives, hypnotics, anesthetics, and anticonvulsants. They produce a drowsy or calming outcome that is beneficial to those suffering from anxiety or sleep disorders, and can be found in tablet, capsule, liquid, or white powder form. Barbiturates were first introduced for medical use in the early 1900s and are a Schedule III drug. Prior to that, CNS depressants existed but had serious side effects.

Benzodiazepines were introduced in the 1960s and were considered safer than earlier depressants. They also held a reduced likelihood for addiction. Of controlled substances, currently one in five is a benzodiazepine.

Unique to the CNS depressant family are those drugs that are used dominantly as animal tranquilizers. Ketamine was created to be used as an animal tranquilizer but had a positive effect on humans. It is still used in some hospitals for humans as an anesthetic, though rarely.

CNS depressants slow normal brain function. The primary differences among many of these products are how fast they produce an effect and how long those effects last. They are swallowed, injected, smoked, or snorted when used illegally. According to the dose, the frequency, and the duration of use, one can rapidly develop tolerance to CNS depressants. As tolerance increases, the amount needed for an effective dose grows in kind. This can come dangerously close to a lethal dose.

According to a 2008 survey, 8.5 percent of students in grade 12 had taken barbiturates at some point. When asked if they had taken "tranquilizers" at some point in their lives, 8.9 percent of students indicated that they had.[8]

Short-term use of CNS depressants can cause confusion, slowed breathing and pulse, and lowered blood pressure. Long-term use can lead to impaired memory, depression, and fatigue. Signs of CNS depressant abuse include slurred speech, impaired coordination and balance, slowed reactions, and changes in motor skills.

Central Nervous System Depressant Fast Facts

 CNS depressants include barbiturates, benzodiazepines, Nembutal, Valium, Librium, Xanax, Halcion, clonezapam, Clonapam, and BNZ. Slang names include *bennies* and *downers*. Benzodiazepines come in a variety of colors, which results in street names such as *yellow jackets*, *reds*, *red birds*, and *blues*.

 Short-term use of CNS depressants can cause poor concentration and judgment, confusion, impaired memory, slowed breathing and pulse, and lowered blood pressure.

 Long-term use of CNS depressants can result in addiction, sleep problems, sexual problems, respiratory depression, and respiratory arrest leading to death.

 Signs associated with CNS depressant abuse include slurred speech, difficulty maintaining balance or impaired coordination, and changes in motor skills. Signs can also include slowed reactions, cognitive inhibition, and changes in thinking or judgment.

Opiates

Opiates are used to treat pain. Though common to many types of medications, opiates are the original drug when referring to narcotics, and they tend to be the most commonly abused prescription among teens. The increase in estimated emergency room visits in relation to opiate use went from 8,232 in 2004 to 22,584 in 2008.[9] Opiates are most common as a white, brown, or black powder, in liquid form, as tablets, or as a patch.

The base plant for opium/opiates is the poppy, which is where the highest abundance of morphine can be found. Morphine is the base substance for many prescription analgesics. (Heroin is also an opiate, but it will be discussed in its own section later.)

OxyContin (a brand name for a time-release version of oxycodone) is a high-profile opiate that was approved for use in 1995. By 2001 it was the best-selling non-generic pain reliever. Hydrocodone is also an opiate with a wide range of popularity. Tablets that have higher dosages of hydrocodone will often also contain acetaminophen, which is a nonaspirin pain reliever. The makers of hydrocodone use the two in tandem to reduce the rates of abuse, as the additional painkiller causes nausea when taken in large quantities.

The addictive qualities of opiates are profound. People of all ages may experience problems when stopping the correctly prescribed use of opiates. Many who find themselves in the struggle to withdraw from use were never in the drug culture and do not have a history of substance abuse. They had not used the analgesic for entertainment but for a physical ailment resulting from an accident, an operation, or a short-term illness. Opiate painkillers are Schedule II drugs.

Short-term side effects include nausea, dry mouth, itching, drowsiness, and impaired mental function. Long-term side effects of opiate use are liver problems and jaundice, impaired mental function and apathy, and an impaired immune system. Signs of opiate abuse include glazed eyes, needle marks, and slurred speech.

Opiate Fast Facts

 Opiates include belladonna, Lortab, Vicodin, OxyContin, hydrocodone, morphine, Tussionex, Olpidem, Ambien, and Percocet. Slang names include *hillbilly heroin*, *OC*, *oxy*, and *Miss Emma*.

 Short-term use of opiates can cause nausea, itching, dry mouth, drowsiness, constipation, and urine retention. Psychological side effects of opiate abuse include impaired mental function, apathy, fatigue, and a feeling of being dissociated from events.

Long-term use of opiates can result in liver problems, weight loss, collapsed veins, pneumonia, and severe addiction and withdrawal symptoms. Since some opiate use requires injections, some opiate abusers face a higher risk of contracting bloodborne diseases such as hepatitis and HIV, and infection of the heart lining and valves.

Signs associated with opiate abuse are impaired coordination, glazed eyes, needle marks, fatigue, and slurred speech.

Anabolic Steroids

Anabolic steroids or anabolic-androgenic steroids are considered Schedule III drugs. Not as much in the limelight as some other prescribed substances, such as opiates and stimulants, they perform a vastly different act. While they can eventually have an effect on the chemical balances of the brain, they work by increasing the levels of testosterone in the blood. This simulates the muscle tissue in the body to grow larger.

Anabolic steroids are a specific formula and not contained in other forms of steroids often prescribed for injuries, allergies, or inflammation. For medical purposes, anabolic steroids treat low levels of testosterone, delayed puberty, and impotence. They have had positive results when used for body wasting linked with breast cancer, AIDS, and other diseases. Forms of anabolic steroids include tablets, capsules, injections (into muscles or the bloodstream), and ointment.

Bodybuilders, athletes, and those just looking to increase body mass by using anabolic steroids are abusing the substance. Anabolic steroids are not a "popular" drug to abuse, but the rate of abuse has remained steady since the early 1990s, with around 2 percent of students in grade 12 reporting that they have taken steroids at some point.[10] While the potential for anabolic steroid abuse is not as pronounced as for some other drugs, addiction behaviors still appear. These behaviors can include spending large amounts of money and continuing to use after social and physical problems appear.

Short-term side effects differ between females and males. Some side effects for girls are facial hair and a deeper voice, while boys can experience shrinking testicles, infertility, and development of breasts. Long-term side effects for both sexes can include liver damage and high blood pressure, blood clotting difficulties, and premature ending of skeletal growth. Signs of steroid abuse include acne, weight gain, increased appetite, abnormal muscle growth patterns, aggression, hostility, and severe mood swings.

Anabolic Steroid Fast Facts

 Anabolic steroids include Anadrol, Oxandrin, Winstrol, Durabolin, and Equipoise. Slang terms are *gym candy*, *stackers*, *roids*, *pumpers*, and *Arnolds*.

 Short-term use of anabolic steroids causes different reactions in men and women. Some side effects for girls are facial hair and a deepening voice. Guys can anticipate shrinking of the testicles, reduced sperm count, infertility, and irreversible development of breasts. Hypertension and fluid retention can occur with either gender.

Long-term use of anabolic steroids can result in liver damage, high blood pressure, and an increased risk for prostate cancer. Other effects are premature termination of growth and skeletal maturation and blood clotting difficulties. Withdrawal symptoms can be very pronounced, and include severe mood swings, reduced sex drive, and depression.

Signs associated with anabolic steroid abuse are acne, rapid weight gain, a change in muscle growth, needle marks over large muscle areas, hair loss that resembles male pattern baldness, and increased appetite. Behaviors include hostility and aggression, mood swings (including manic symptoms leading to violence), impaired judgment, depression, nervousness, extreme irritability, delusions, hostility, and aggression.

References

1. National Institute on Drug Abuse, "NIDA InfoFacts: Cigarettes and Other Tobacco Products," Bethesda, MD: NIDA, NIH, DHHS. Revised June 2009. www.nida.nih.gov/infofacts/tobacco.html.

2. National Institute on Drug Abuse, "NIDA for Teens: The Science Behind Drug Abuse," Bethesda, MD: NIDA, NIH, DHHS. Revised June 2009. teens.drugabuse.gov/facts/facts_nicotine1.php.

3. Centers for Disease Control and Prevention, "Smoking and Tobacco Use—Fact Sheet: Health Effects of Cigarette Smoking," Atlanta, GA: National Center for Chronic Disease Prevention and Health Promotion, December 2009. www.cdc.gov/tobacco/data_statistics/fact_sheets/health_effects/effects_cig_smoking.

4. Paul Vallely, "2,000 Years of Binge Drinking," *Independent*, November 19, 2005.

5. Centers for Disease Control and Prevention, "Youth Risk Behavior Surveillance—United States, 2009," *Surveillance Summaries*, MMWR 2010; 59 (No. SS-5905), Atlanta, GA: National Center for Chronic Disease Prevention and Health Promotion, June 4, 2010. www.cdc.gov/mmwr/PDF/ss/ss5905.pdf.

6. National Association of Boards of Pharmacy, *NABP Internet Drug Outlet Report*, Mount Prospect, IL: NABP, 2010.

7. L. D. Johnston, P. M. O'Malley, J. G. Bachman, and J. E. Schulenberg, *Monitoring the Future: National Survey Results on Drug Use, 1975–2008: Volume I, Secondary School Students* (NIH Publication No. 09-7402), Bethesda, MD: National Institute on Drug Abuse, 2009.

8. Ibid.

9. Drug Abuse Warning Network, "2008: Selected Tables of National Estimates of Drug-Related Emergency Department Visits," Rockville, MD: Office of Applied Studies, SAMHSA, 2009.

10. Johnston et al., *Monitoring the Future*.

Chapter 9

Illegal Substances

ILLEGAL SUBSTANCES DON'T USUALLY START OUT THAT WAY. MOST AT one time had medicinal purposes but are no longer in use due to their lack of safety or because other substances have come along that are more effective. Heroin, cocaine, and various club drugs and hallucinogens have all been used in the past to treat medical disorders—and before the days of government oversight, cocaine and heroin in particular were "special ingredients" in many patent medicines.

Abuse of illegal (or controlled) drugs such as cocaine, methamphetamine, and heroin is not as common as the abuse of more easily accessible substances. Teens have easy access to alcohol, prescription drugs, household chemicals, and over-the-counter medications, and the percentage of youth who abuse these substances is far higher than the percentage of teens who abuse what society tends to think of as "real" drugs.[1] Marijuana, however, is the exception to this rule.

Marijuana/Cannabis/THC

Though marijuana is classified as illegal (medical marijuana is available in a few U.S. states), it is much easier to procure and use than substances such as heroin or cocaine. Because of this availability, marijuana ranks second as the most abused drug for youth in middle and high school.[2] Alcohol remains at the top.

Marijuana is made up of the shredded leaves, stems, and seeds from dried cannabis—a flowering blue-green plant with five spiky leaves that dries to a dull green, brown, or gray color. It is usually smoked, either in cigarette papers, in a pipe, or through a water pipe (bong or hookah), but it can also be ingested in food, and it comes in varying levels of potency. Hashish or hash is another substance derived from cannabis and is created from the flower of the female cannabis plant. It is usually smoked, and it is typically stronger than marijuana.

Cannabis produces male and female plants, and both of them contain delta-9-tetrahydrocannabinol or THC. THC is the main mind-altering chemical in marijuana. Female plants contain the highest concentrations of THC, and both male and female plants are necessary for proper pollination.

Cannabis use was legal until the 1930s, and there has been consistent debate over the effects of its use and its addictive powers. As with any drug, there have been careful studies to show the value of use and the problems associated with misuse. Studies show that the potential positive attributes of marijuana use do not overpower the threat of harm. The marijuana of today is five times more potent than it was in the 1970s, but the parents of today's youth could have been marijuana users during their own teen years, which can result in a wider tolerance for use.[3]

A National Institute on Drug Abuse–funded, 2009 *Monitoring the Future* study showed that 10.9 percent of students in grade 8, 23.9 percent of grade 10 students, and 32.4 percent of grade 12 students had abused marijuana at least once in the year prior to being surveyed. Marijuana use among American adolescents has been increasing gradually over the past two years (three years among grade 12 students) following years of declining use.[4]

Long-term marijuana use leads to addiction in some people. As with any form of addiction, use negatively affects family relationships, school performance, and recreational activities. While scientists are still learning about how THC affects the brain, they have found that smoking marijuana causes some changes in the brain that are similar to those caused by other drugs.

Spice and K2 are rapidly becoming a substitute for marijuana. They are incense blends that, when smoked, have the same effect as marijuana, though they contain no THC. This is a good example of a concept I mentioned at the start of the book: people will always attempt new things to get high.

Side effects of Spice and K2 use are very similar to THC use, but because it has been available only since the mid-1990s, the long-term effects from use are still unknown.

Marijuana Fast Facts

 Marijuana is also called *weed, skunkweed, pot, hemp, Mary Jane, reefer, grass, ganja, hash, bud, dope, and sensimilla.*

 Short-term use of marijuana can result in memory impairment, difficulty concentrating, and delayed reactions. Confusion and "cloudy" perception are also short-term side effects. Verbal skills and judgment can be affected, and increased appetite can occur.

Long-term use of marijuana can cause respiratory issues and other problems similar to those caused by tobacco use. Some studies show that when people have smoked large amounts of marijuana for years, the drug affects mental functions. Heavy or daily use of marijuana affects the parts of the brain that control memory, attention, and learning.

Signs associated with marijuana abuse include bloodshot eyes, fatigue, lack of concentration, extreme hunger followed by extreme lack of hunger, slow reaction time, and the appearance of being intoxicated.

Club Drugs

. . . .

Club drugs are commonly found at nightclubs, bars, and raves—hence their name. Some common club drugs are Rohypnol, GHB, ketamine, and MDMA (ecstasy, E, or X). Methamphetamine is also sometimes used as a club drug, but will be discussed separately. Rohypnol, GHB, and ketamine are from the central nervous system (CNS) depressant family (discussed in more detail in Chapter 8), while MDMA is a stimulant. Club drugs are generally low in cost. They are often made in clandestine or illegal labs, and the manufacturing process can release toxins into the environment. Medical consequences may arise that cannot be traced back to the club drug itself, but rather to the pollutants created by its manufacture.

Rohypnol is a depressant similar to Valium and is illegal in the United States. Rohypnol is usually taken orally, although there are reports that it can be ground up and snorted. GHB is a depressant that was originally used for sleeping disorders and as an anesthetic. GHB also has performance-enhancing effects (like anabolic steroids) and is sought by bodybuilders.

Rohypnol and GHB have both been called "the date rape drug": they are colorless, tasteless, odorless, and can be dissolved in liquid; those who take them may not remember their experience while under the influence; and they can render the user (the victim in this case) unable to resist an aggressor.

Ketamine was created to be used as an animal tranquilizer but is used in some hospitals as a human anesthetic. It has a dissociative effect, meaning that those who use it feel detached from their surroundings. Ketamine is usually snorted or injected.

Short-term use of Rohypnol, GHB, and ketamine can cause poor concentration and judgment, confusion, depression, and impaired memory. Longer use is indicated by slowed breathing and lowered blood pressure, but club drugs are not generally taken for sustained periods of time. Signs of Rohypnol, GHB, and ketamine abuse are slurred speech, staggering, poor concentration, and changes in motor skills. Users can also have difficulty maintaining balance or coordination and experience slowed reactions, cognitive inhibition, and changes in thinking, judgment, and motor skills.

On the other side of the club drug spectrum, MDMA, or ecstasy, can induce psychedelic hallucinations and act as a stimulant. MDMA is derived from an essential oil of the sassafras tree but must go through a complex manufacturing process to reach final tablet form. Its side effects include lack of appetite, insomnia, and tremors. Signs of its use may include impaired speech, dilated pupils, rapid respiration, and profuse sweating in the short term, and restlessness and weight loss in the long term.

Club Drugs Fast Facts

Other Names for Club Drugs

Rohypnol is sometimes referred to as a *roofie*.

GHB slang names include *cherry meth, easy lay, G, Georgia homeboy, G-riffick, liquid ecstasy* (not the same as the drug ecstasy), *liquid E, liquid X, salty dog, salty water, scoop, soap,* and *zonked*.

Ketamine can be called *cat Valium, honey oil, jet, kit kat, special K,* and *vitamin K*.

Other names for **MDMA** are *E, X, ecstasy,* and *XTC*.

Short-term use of GHB, Rohypnol, and ketamine can cause poor concentration and judgment, confusion, depression, and impaired memory. Longer use is indicated by slowed breathing and lowered blood pressure. **Short-term use of MDMA** can cause nausea, chills, teeth clenching, insomnia, and loss of appetite.

Long-term use of GHB, Rohypnol, ketamine, and MDMA can result in depression, sleep disorders, persistent anxiety, and memory loss.

Signs associated with GHB, Rohypnol, and ketamine abuse are slurred speech, staggering, poor concentration, and changes in motor skills. Other signs can be difficulty maintaining balance, impaired coordination, slowed reactions, cognitive inhibition, and changes in thinking, judgment, and motor skills.

Signs associated with MDMA abuse include dilated pupils, rapid respiration, profuse sweating, and a runny nose. Behaviors may include restlessness, confusion, panic, inability to concentrate, incessant talking, and insomnia. Long-term signs of use include weight loss and sleeplessness.

Cocaine

Cocaine hydrochloride is a fine powder derived from the coca plant and is a stimulant as well as an anesthetic. It can be snorted, smoked, or diluted with water and injected. A crystalline "rock" form of cocaine, called crack, can be heated in a pipe and inhaled (the term *crack* comes from the crackling sound the crystals make as they are heated). Cocaine use among youth has seen a steady decline since the 1990s.[5]

A cocaine "high" is an immediate euphoric effect that includes energy, reduced fatigue, and mental clarity, depending on how it is used. The high from cocaine does not last long, however, and the faster it is absorbed, the more intense but shorter the high. Absorption by injecting, for example, will give a more intense high but will not last as long as snorting powder. The aftereffects of use are called a "crash," and include depression, irritability, and fatigue. Abusers will use cocaine in binges to sustain the high, often until they either run out of money or become unconscious.

Short-term use of cocaine and crack cocaine can lead to insomnia, loss of appetite, and feelings of restlessness, irritability, and anxiety. Cocaine use causes blood vessels to constrict and increase body temperature, heart rate, and blood pressure, which puts a short-term strain on the heart. Long-term effects include difficulty with verbal communication and memory issues, as well as prolonged intestinal or nose and throat illness.

The method of cocaine use has additional health risks. Irritation of the nasal cavities and other nose and throat issues are common side effects of snorting cocaine. Swallowing cocaine can cause intestinal problems.

As with many drugs, users develop a tolerance and so must consume more to achieve the same effect. Some users seek to re-create the feeling from their first high, though the effects of the original experience are usually never matched. "Chasing" this high can lead to chronic addiction or overdose. Some users will increase their dose in an attempt to intensify and prolong the euphoria, but this can also increase the risk of adverse psychological or physiological effects.

Cocaine Fast Facts

 Cocaine is also called *crack*, *C*, *coke*, *dust*, *nose candy*, *rock*, *white lines*, and *blow*.

Short-term use of cocaine can lead to insomnia, loss of appetite, feelings of restlessness, irritability, and anxiety. Cocaine use causes constricted blood vessels, dilated pupils, and increased body temperature, heart rate, and blood pressure.

Long-term use of cocaine is the same as with many stimulants: higher doses result in fever, an unusually fast heartbeat, chest pain, blurred vision, tics, tremors, and antisocial behavior. Someone who is using stimulants may have psychological side effects such as agitation, aggression, hostility, and panic. Chronic use may result in dry and itchy skin, convulsions, a strong sense of paranoia, and hallucinations. Suicidal or homicidal tendencies can also be part of stimulant side effects. Abuse can mimic schizophrenia, such as delusions, hallucinations, disordered thinking, and a sensation of distance from one's environment.

Signs associated with cocaine abuse can include dilated pupils, rapid respiration, profuse sweating, a runny nose, and being underweight. Other signs include sores, a flushed face, mouth and gum problems, uncontrollable movements or shaking, facial itching, and needle marks. Behaviors include restlessness, confusion, panic, an inability to concentrate, and being secretive. Other strong behavior changes can include agitation or defensiveness, uncontrolled movement or shaking, frequent absences, isolation and withdrawal, and mood swings.

Hallucinogens

. . . .

Types of hallucinogens include lysergic acid (LSD), peyote, psilocybin, and phency-clidine (PCP). Hallucinogens distort a person's awareness of the surrounding environment. People on hallucinogens will feel, see, and hear things that aren't there, believe their distorted view of reality is truth, and experience intense mood swings. Hallucinogens such as LSD, peyote, and psilocybin interrupt the normal control of behavior, while PCP, due to its anesthetic properties, disrupts reactions to physical stimuli and dulls pain. Hallucinogens are not normally the drug of choice among teens today.[6]

LSD is sold in tablets, capsules, and sometimes as a liquid, and is ingested. An LSD "trip" can last up to 12 hours. The effects of a trip are not under the control of the user: reactions can range from euphoria and pleasure to sensations of fear and panic, loss of control, and feeling trapped. While there may not be any actual physical change during a trip, users have told stories of altered states of senses. The effects of LSD depend largely on the amount taken.

Peyote is "a small, spineless cactus in which the principal active ingredient is mescaline."[7] Peyote "buttons," so called because of their disklike shape, are found on the top of the peyote cactus. After they are dried, peyote buttons can be chewed, boiled into a tea, or the mescaline can be extracted through soaking. The effects are similar to those of LSD and also last about 12 hours. Not all peyote use is illegal, however. The consumption of peyote for spiritual purposes has been part of many Native American traditions for thousands of years, and members of the Native American Church are legally allowed to import, possess, and use it for religious ceremonies.

Psilocybin is obtained from certain types of mushrooms that are found in South America, Mexico, and the United States. Mushrooms containing psilocybin are eaten alone or added to food. The effects of "magic mushrooms" are about half as long as those of LSD and peyote, meaning the change in consciousness lasts about six hours.

PCP was originally developed as an anesthetic but was discontinued for human use in the 1960s after multiple adverse reactions. It continues to be used as a veterinary tranquilizer. PCP is a white crystalline powder that can be smoked, snorted, or dissolved in water or alcohol. Its negative post-high side effects have kept it from being a commonly abused substance. As with mushrooms, the effects of PCP can last up to six hours.

Hallucinogen Fast Facts

☑ **Hallucinogens are known as** *LSD*, *acid*, *mellow yellow*, *blotter acid* (LSD added to absorbent paper), *mescaline*, *cactus*, *shrooms*, *peyote buttons*, *psilocybin/psilocin*, and *Mexican mushrooms*. PCP can be called *angel dust*, *hog*, *rocket fuel*, *peace pill*, and *DOA*.

☑ **Short-term use of LSD, peyote, and psilocybin mushrooms** can cause a rise in temperature and increased heart rate and blood pressure. It can also cause a loss of appetite, sleeplessness, and dry mouth. Rapid emotional changes, delusions, and hallucinations are also effects of use. **PCP** causes effects that vary according to dosage and the individual, and can act as a stimulant, a depressant, an analgesic, or a hallucinogen. Slurred or jumbled speech, confusion, severe hallucinations, and delirium are common effects.

☑ **Long-term use of hallucinogens** can cause flashbacks, personality changes, memory impairment, and drug-induced psychosis lasting several hours.

☑ **Signs associated with hallucinogen use** are sweating, uncontrolled movement, dilated pupils, a redness of the skin, and tremors. Some stronger doses will produce erratic behavior and actions.

Side effects of LSD, peyote, and psilocybin use can be a rise in body temperature, increased heart rate, and increased blood pressure. In addition, loss of appetite, sleeplessness, and dry mouth may also appear, as well as rapid emotional changes, delusions, and hallucinations. PCP side effects are similar to those of other anesthetics and include a sense of dissociation and absence of pain; reactions after a trip may include irrational and agitated behavior.

A long-term effect of hallucinogen use can be flashbacks. In this case, a flashback is the repetition of a prior hallucinogen experience after an extended period of time. They have been known to occur months after use. Signs of hallucinogen use are sweating, uncontrolled movement, dilated pupils, a redness of the skin, and tremors.

Methamphetamine

. . . .

Methamphetamine is a stimulant. It can be prescribed by a doctor in small amounts that are usually lower than what's required for abuse. In its raw and illegal form, it is a white to light brown or gray saltlike powder. It can be snorted, smoked as a powder, or dissolved in liquid and injected. Methamphetamine's ability to work quickly on the brain produces intense euphoria, and the changes it causes in brain chemistry, beginning at the first use, can cause immediate addiction issues. Methamphetamine addiction has a recovery rate of over two years, on average.

Those who make and abuse meth form a sort of subculture that can be hard to break away from. Meth users are often much more involved in the manufacturing process compared to those who abuse cocaine or heroin. Because "cooking" meth doesn't require highly specialized equipment or advanced knowledge of chemistry, it can be produced in homes, apartments, garages, barns, and cars using over-the-counter substances. Some of these substances have strict purchasing limits, so getting enough ingredients for meth production usually requires a number of people. Still more people are needed to procure necessary materials, provide space, and cook the actual product. They all work meticulously as a community to produce the drug.

A local "meth lab" endangers the people in the lab, those who live in the building, their neighbors, and the environment. Production of meth creates fumes and byproducts that are absorbed into flooring and drywall; this residue contains active ingredients that can affect those living in the home the same way it affects the actual abuser. Buildings that have housed labs must be carefully cleaned according to strict regulations before they are deemed habitable again. However, methamphetamine production has been gradually moving from very small, localized labs to foreign and domestic "super labs" (meaning they produce more than 10 pounds of meth during a production cycle).[8]

The side effects of meth include a decrease in appetite, rapid breathing, an increase in heart rate, anxiety, and confusion. The long-term abuse of meth results in many negative health consequences, such as severe dental problems ("meth mouth"), extreme weight loss, severe paranoia, fear, and displaced aggression. Signs of meth use include scratching and digging at the arms and legs, bad breath, rotting teeth, and a lack of attention to personal hygiene.

Methamphetamine Fast Facts

 Methamphetamine is called *meth, crystal meth, crank, ice, stove top, chalk, glass, poor man's cocaine, shabu, tina, trash,* and *zip.*

 Short-term use of methamphetamine results in symptoms similar to other stimulants, such as an irregular heartbeat, rapid heartbeat, and increased breathing rates and blood pressure. Insomnia, anxiety, confusion, and decreased appetite are also associated with meth use.

 Long-term use of methamphetamine has many negative health consequences such as severe dental problems referred to as "meth mouth." Emotional and mental issues include severe paranoia and fear, visual and auditory hallucinations, and homicidal or suicidal thoughts. Psychotic symptoms may persist long after meth use ceases.

Signs associated with methamphetamine abusers include sudden weight loss, inattentiveness and confusion, and scratching and digging at areas of arms and legs. Sleeplessness followed by long periods of sleep is common. After prolonged use, rotting teeth and bad breath and a foul chemical odor can appear.

Heroin

Heroin is an opiate drug created from morphine. Opiate drugs are predominantly used to provide serious pain relief. In powder form, heroin ranges in color from white to dark brown. It can also be found as a hard black sticky material known as tar heroin. Heroin is most likely to be snorted, smoked, or injected.

Heroin use among youth has historically been low. The latest *Monitoring the Future* survey puts the rate of use at less than 1 percent among students in grades 8, 10, and 12.[9] There is some evidence that this rate is growing: the 2008 National Survey on Drug Use and Health indicated that heroin use among youth aged 12 and older increased by nearly 40 percent from 2007 levels, but more surveys are needed to determine whether that is a statistical anomaly.[10]

Use of heroin produces an immediate euphoria. After the initial rush, users enter a state of drowsiness, called being "on the nod," and mental functions slow, along with heart rate and breathing. Injecting heroin creates a more intense reaction than smoking or snorting it. Short-term side effects include nausea, vomiting, and severe itching, while long-term side effects can include damage to the heart, liver and kidney disease, and the development of certain pneumonias. Signs of heroin use include scratching, impaired mental function, delayed reaction time, and contracted pupils.

Heroin Fast Facts

 Heroin is also known as *big H, china white, Mexican brown, smack, antifreeze, Aunt Hazel, H, Harry, big Harry, black pearl, black tar, brain damage, brown sugar, diesel,* and *tootsie roll.*

 Short-term use of heroin can cause a flushed feeling and a sensation of heaviness in the extremities. Heart rate and breathing slow, and mental function is reduced. Heroin use can also cause nausea, vomiting, and severe itching.

Long-term use of heroin can result in bacterial infections and abscesses as well as liver and kidney disease. Lung issues such as certain pneumonias may develop due to decreases in breathing rates. Since heroin requires injections, abusers face a higher risk of contracting bloodborne diseases such as hepatitis and HIV, and infection of the heart lining and valves.

Signs associated with heroin abuse include itching, euphoria, impaired mental function, contracted pupils, and slowed reaction time.

References

1. L. D. Johnston, P. M. O'Malley, J. G. Bachman, and J. E. Schulenberg, *Monitoring the Future: National Survey Results on Drug Use, 1975–2008: Volume I, Secondary School Students* (NIH Publication No. 09-7402), Bethesda, MD: National Institute on Drug Abuse, 2009.

2. Ibid.

3. National Institute on Drug Abuse, "Research Report Series: Marijuana Abuse," NIH Publication Number 05-3859, Bethesda, MD: NIDA, NIH, DHHS, 2010. www.drugabuse.gov/PDF/RRMarijuana.pdf.

4. Johnston et al., *Monitoring the Future.*

5. Ibid.

6. Ibid.

7. National Institute on Drug Abuse, "NIDA InfoFacts: Hallucinogens—LSD, Peyote, Psilocybin, and PCP," Bethesda, MD: NIDA, NIH, DIIIIS. Revised June 2009. www.drugabuse.gov/Infofacts/hallucinogens.html.

8. National Drug Intelligence Center, "Methamphetamine Drug Threat Assessment," March 2005. www.justice.gov/ndic/pubs11/13853/product.htm.

9. Johnston et al., *Monitoring the Future.*

10. Substance Abuse and Mental Health Services Administration, *Results from the 2008 National Survey on Drug Use and Health: National Findings* (Office of Applied Studies, NSDUH Series H-36, HHS Publication No. SMA 09-4434), Rockville, MD: SAMHSA, 2009.

Bibliography

American Medical Association. "Adults Most Common Source of Alcohol for Teens, According to Poll of Teens 13–18." *Alcohol Policy MD*, August 8, 2005. www.alcoholpolicymd.com/press_room/Press_releases/adults_give_youth_alcohol.htm.

Arthur, M. W., J. D. Hawkins, J. A. Pollard, R. Catalano, and A. J. Baglioni Jr. "Measuring Risk and Protective Factors for Substance Use, Delinquency, and Other Adolescent Problem Behaviors." *Evaluation Review* 26, no. 6, 575–601, 2002.

Breyer, Jessie, and Ken C. Winters. "Adolescent Brain Development: Implications for Drug Use Prevention." Minneapolis: Center for Substance Abuse Research, Department of Psychiatry, University of Minnesota & Mentor USA, 2004. www.mentorfoundation.org/pdfs/prevention_perspectives/19.pdf.

Centers for Disease Control and Prevention. "2009 National Youth Risk Behavior Survey Overview." National Center for Chronic Disease Prevention and Health Promotion, 2009. www.cdc.gov/HealthyYouth/yrbs/pdf/us_overview_yrbs.pdf.

———. "Smoking and Tobacco Use—Fact Sheet: Health Effects of Cigarette Smoking." Atlanta, GA: National Center for Chronic Disease Prevention and Health Promotion, December 2009. www.cdc.gov/tobacco/data_statistics/fact_sheets/health_effects/effects_cig_smoking.

———. "Youth Risk Behavior Surveillance—United States, 2009." *Surveillance Summaries*, MMWR 2010; 59 (No. SS-5905). Atlanta, GA: National Center for Chronic Disease Prevention and Health Promotion, June 4, 2010. www.cdc.gov/mmwr/PDF/ss/ss5905.pdf.

Drug Abuse Warning Network. "2008: Selected Tables of National Estimates of Drug-Related Emergency Department Visits." Rockville, MD: Office of Applied Studies, SAMHSA, 2009.

Gassman, R., M. K. Jun, S. Samuel, J. D. Agley, J. A. Swanson, J. Lee, B. D. Agley, S. M. Conley, T. R. Gray, A. M. Holt, E. E. King, E. A. Laine, D. G. Mart, S. E. Oi, B. J. Olsen, S. E. Pardue, M. J. Richard, M. D. Smith, U. Tripathi, and L. E. Zvolner, *Alcohol, Tobacco, and Other Drug Use by Indiana Children and Adolescents: The Indiana Prevention Resource Center Survey-2010* (IDAP Monograph No. 10-01). Bloomington: Indiana Prevention Resource Center, 2010.

Hawkins, J. D., R. F. Catalano, and J. Y. Miller. "Risk and Protective Factors for Alcohol and Other Drug Problems in Adolescence and Early Adulthood: Implications for Substance Abuse Prevention." *Psychological Bulletin* 12, 64–105, 1992.

Indiana Prevention Resource Center. "Indiana Youth Survey: Annual Monograph." August 2009. www.drugs.indiana.edu.

Johnston, L. D., P. M. O'Malley, J. G. Bachman, and J. E. Schulenberg. *Monitoring the Future: National Survey Results on Drug Use, 1975–2008: Volume I, Secondary School Students* (NIH Publication No. 09-7402). Bethesda, MD: National Institute on Drug Abuse, 2009.

National Association of Boards of Pharmacy. *NABP Internet Drug Outlet Report.* Mount Prospect, IL: NABP, 2010.

National Drug Intelligence Center. "Intelligence Bulletin: DXM (Dextromethorphan)." Document ID: 2004-L0424-029. October 2004.

——. "Methamphetamine Drug Threat Assessment." March 2005. www.justice.gov/ndic/pubs11/13853/product.htm.

National Institute on Drug Abuse. "NIDA for Teens: The Science Behind Drug Abuse." Bethesda, MD: NIDA, NIH, DHHS. Revised June 2009. teens.drugabuse.gov/facts/facts_nicotine1.php.

——. "NIDA InfoFacts: Cigarettes and Other Tobacco Products." Bethesda, MD: NIDA, NIH, DHHS. Revised June 2009. www.nida.nih.gov/infofacts/tobacco.html.

——. "NIDA InfoFacts: Hallucinogens—LSD, Peyote, Psilocybin, and PCP." Bethesda, MD: NIDA, NIH, DHHS. Revised June 2009. www.drugabuse.gov/Infofacts/hallucinogens.html.

——. "Research Report Series: Marijuana Abuse." NIH Publication Number 05-3859. Bethesda, MD: NIDA, NIH, DHHS, 2005. www.drugabuse.gov/PDF/RRMarijuana.pdf.

Partnership for a Drug Free America. "DXM Abuse Warning." May 15, 2006. www.drugfree.org/Portal/DrugIssue/News/DXM_Abuse_Warning.

Schedules of Controlled Substances. U.S. Code. Vol. 21, sec. 812 (2009).

Substance Abuse and Mental Health Services Administration. "Nonmedical Use of Adderall among Full Time College Students." *NSDUH Report,* April 7, 2009. www.oas.samhsa.gov/2k9/adderall/adderall.htm.

———. *The NSDUH Report: Trends in Adolescent Inhalant Use: 2002 to 2007*. Rockville, MD: SAMHSA, 2009.

———. *Results from the 2008 National Survey on Drug Use and Health: National Findings* (Office of Applied Studies, NSDUH Series H-36, HHS Publication No. SMA 09-4434). Rockville, MD: SAMHSA, 2009.

Vallely, Paul. "2,000 Years of Binge Drinking." *Independent*. November 19, 2005.

Werthamer, Lisa, and Pinka Chatterji. *Prevention Intervention Cost-Effectiveness and Cost Benefit Literature Review*. Bethesda, MD: National Institute of Drug Abuse, 2008.

Further Resources

Websites

Keep Rx Safe: keeprxsafe.com

Parents. The Anti-Drug: www.theantidrug.com

The Office of National Drug Control Policy: www.whitehousedrugpolicy.gov

The National Institute on Drug Abuse: drugabuse.gov/nidahome.html

The Canadian Centre on Substance Abuse: www.ccsa.ca

Evidence-Based School or After-School Programs

Evidence-based programs are those that have been proved successful in a number of different demographics and environments. There are hundreds of programs available for use. However, not all are adaptable for your particular environment. Be certain the studies reflect those students who will be served. You can find a full list of evidence-based programs at the National Registry of Evidence-Based Programs and Practices: www.nrepp.samhsa.gov. For a list of successful Canadian programs, go to "School-Based Drug Abuse Prevention: Promising and Successful Programs," at www.publicsafety.gc.ca/res/cp/res/2009-01-drg-abs-eng.aspx.

AlcoholEdu for High School is an online, interactive, alcohol education and prevention course designed to increase alcohol-related knowledge, discourage acceptance of underage drinking, and prevent or decrease alcohol use and its related negative consequences. **www.outsidetheclassroom.com**

Project Northland is a multilevel intervention involving students, peers, parents, and community in programs designed to delay the age at which adolescents begin drinking, reduce alcohol use among those already drinking, and limit the number of alcohol-related problems among young drinkers. **www.hazelden.org/web/go/ projectnorthland**

Class Action is the second phase of the Project Northland alcohol-use prevention curriculum series. Class Action (for grades 11 and 12) and Project Northland (for grades 6 through 8) are designed to delay the onset of alcohol use, reduce use among youths who have already tried alcohol, and limit the number of alcohol-related problems experienced by young drinkers. **www.hazelden.org**

PRIME For Life (PFL) is a motivational intervention used in group settings to prevent alcohol and drug problems or provide early intervention. PFL has been used primarily among court-referred impaired driving offenders. **www.primeforlife.org**

The Strengthening Families Program (SFP) is a family skills training program designed to increase resilience and reduce risk factors for behavioral, emotional, academic, and social problems in children 3 to 16 years old. **www.strengthening familiesprogram.org**

The WhyTry Program is a strength-based approach to helping youth overcome their challenges and improve outcomes in the areas of truancy, behavior, and academics. It is based on sound, empirical principles, including Solution Focused Brief Therapy, Social and Emotional Intelligence, and multisensory learning. **www.why try.org**

Brief Alcohol Screening and Intervention for College Students (BASICS) is a prevention program for college students who drink alcohol heavily and have experienced or are at risk for alcohol-related problems. **depts.washington.edu/abrc/ basics.htm**

Index

About the Author

Katharine Sadler is a community prevention specialist who has worked as a teacher, school counselor, business executive, and community activist. She is with Indiana Prevention Resource Center at Indiana University as a technical assistant and evaluator for prevention projects. Her understanding of the substance abuse culture also stems from seeing it firsthand as a school administrator and as a mom. Katharine resides in Elizabeth, Indiana.

About Search Institute Press

Search Institute Press is a division of Search Institute, a nonprofit organization that offers leadership, knowledge, and resources to promote positive youth development. Our mission at Search Institute Press is to provide practical and hope-filled resources to help create a world in which all young people thrive. Our products are embedded in research, and the 40 Developmental Assets®—qualities, experiences, and relationships youth need to succeed—are a central focus of our resources. Our logo, the SIP flower, is a symbol of the thriving and healthy growth young people experience when they have an abundance of assets in their lives.